Korean Combat

The Four Freedoms Betrayed

A Fighter Pilot's Diary

Captain David Leue' USN (Ret)

About the author

Captain David Leue' joined the Navy while a senior at Buffalo Technical High School. In his thirty-two year naval career he moved through the ranks from Apprentice Seaman to Captain. As a fighter/attack pilot he survived 329 combat missions flying from the decks of the aircraft carriers USS Boxer, USS Valley Forge, USS Philippine Sea, USS Coral Sea and USS Constellation, fighting for freedom in Korea and Vietnam.

Significant commands were: Commander Carrier Air Wing Seven; Squadron Commander Attack Squadron One Fifty-Three; Captain of USS Canisteo AO-99, a 650 foot armed replenishment ship; Chief of Staff Carrier Group Three; and Chief of Staff, Light Attack Wing, Pacific at NAS Lemoore, California.

His education includes the Armed Forces Staff College, a Bachelor of Science in Physics from the University of California at Berkeley and a Master's of Science in Engineering/Industrial Technology, California State University, Fresno, emphasizing solar energy.

Following naval service, he established Leue' Solar Inc., designing and installing many unique solar systems in the San Joaquin Valley. He then served as Professor of Engineering/Construction Management, California State University Fresno followed by twenty years as an Engineer with Pacific Gas & Electric working on energy efficiency projects in the food and agriculture industry.

Contents

Korean Combat

	PAGE
CONTENTS	
DEDICATIONS AND ACKNOWLEDGEMENTS	v
PREFACE	vi
CHAPTERS	
1. First Combat	1
2. Navy V-5 College Program	17
3. Pensacola, Basic Training	33
4. Advanced Training	59
5. Carrier Qualifications	83
6. Fighter Squadron 24	93
7. USS Valley Forge	114
8. USS Philippine Sea	140
9. Marriage, Panther Jets	160
10. USS Boxer, 1952	177
11. The Four Freedoms Betrayed	202
BIBLIOGRAPHY	208
APPENDIX A FDR's "Four Freedoms" Speech	1A

Dedications and Acknowledgements

Dedication

This book is dedicated to my Carrier Air Group Two shipmates who gave their lives in the cause of freedom for the Korean people.

Acknowledgments

The mentoring, critiques and encouragement of Janice Stevens and her Writers for Publication Group were key in developing my skills and guiding me through the completion of this book. The professional editing of Monica Stevens, my daughter Rebecca Roth, my sons Paul Leue' and Mark Hinds and my wife Stella Leue' were all critical to the book's high quality. The excellent photos provided by my Air Group Two shipmate, Bill Crouse, greatly enhance the manuscript.

Preface

Hidden History

Born in 1928, clearly, the events and attitudes of the Great Depression shaped my childhood. However, the cares and concerns of those dark days were dramatically swept away by the Japanese attack on Pearl Harbor.

President Roosevelt, Winston Churchill and Joseph Stalin, were portrayed in our press as great men, fighting for freedom. I watched as my older classmates went off to fight in World War II. Finally, in the Spring of 1945, as a Junior attending Buffalo Technical High School, I received "Greetings" from the Buffalo Draft Board and was classified "1A, Fit for Duty."

Naively, I was eager to go. However, my class, the Class of 1946, was spared fighting in the invasion of Japan. The Atomic bombings of Hiroshima and Nagasaki, in August 1945 saved us.

The world looked forward to endless peace and freedom. I planned to join the Navy, learn to fly, get an education and hoped to become an airline pilot.

Unknown to most, and of no concern to me, our WWII ally, Joseph Stalin, had other ideas.

Thanks to the U.S. press, Edward R. Morrow and friends, I, and the country were led to believe Stalin was our best friend. My lessons in the real world began only after naval flight training, joining Fighter Squadron 24 in Carrier Air Group Two. I would fly one hundred missions in battles fighting the North Korean and Chinese communists in Korea. This would alter my view of the world, forever.

The descriptions of combat, remembrances of shipmates and historical events in these pages are based on my aviation log books, carrier cruise-books, my recollections, those of my shipmates, and extensive research concerning Stalin, FDR,

Preface

Churchill and WWII.

I was privileged to fly two great Navy fighter planes, the F4U-4 Corsair and the F9F-2 Panther, from the decks of the USS Boxer, USS Valley Forge, and USS Philippine Sea fighting for the freedom of the South Korean people.

The Korean War wasn't a glamorous war. It was fought against our WWII ally, the newly emerging aggressor, Stalin and International Communism. During the Korean War newspaper and radio correspondents were confused. Five years earlier they had praised Stalin. Was the country just "war weary" or did the press still harbor lingering support for the Soviets and their great leader?

Carrier Air Group Two fought in Korea for almost three years, predominately against the Chinese. Our Air Wing lost one-third of its embarked aircraft and pilots and crew to accurate, concentrated anti-aircraft weapons, fires at sea, and the ever present dangers of operating high performance aircraft flying from carriers at sea. Our mission was to carry the weapons of war and use them to good effect in support of hard-fighting U.S. Marine, Army and U.N. troops in the mud below. The country and the press were generally indifferent to our exploits.

The closing chapter is an examination of the origins of the Korean War in light of a forgotten key event in history, President Franklin Roosevelt's pre-Pearl Harbor "Four Freedoms" speech. In this speech FDR stated, "we must fight THE DICTATORS," which in January 1941, included Hitler <u>and</u> Stalin.

Did President Roosevelt betray his own historic words by arming Stalin, a known tyrant, taking him as an ally, instead of defeating him along with Hitler?

David E. Leue'

Chapter One

First Combat

Suspense

September 10, 1950. The USS Boxer sped at 26 knots toward the west coast of Korea in the Yellow Sea. Tension continued to build. I couldn't help speculate, what would combat be like? How would I perform?

USS Boxer, Armed & Ready B. Crouse

I recalled an incident when I was ten years old. We were living on Balboa Island, California. My small rowboat had recently been stolen. My father had found my rowboat on a locked private dock on the other side of the island. He told me, "Get your oars, climb over that fence, get in your boat and row it home."

I was scared. I said to myself, "How could I ever be a soldier, or go to war?"

Well, twelve years later I was Ensign Dave Leue,' Corsair pilot, Fighter Squadron Twenty Four, Carrier Air Group Two, USS Boxer. I was about to find out. My heart beat at an advanced rate. My chest hurt.

Inchon

The Korean War began June 25, 1950, when the North Koreans attacked South Korea without warning. With the help of Russia and China, North Korean forces quickly overran Seoul, the capital, then rapidly pushed the faltering South Korean army south. The hasty deployment of poorly trained U.S. peacetime troops from Japan, aided by scattered United Nations forces, failed to stem the Red Tide.

By September 1950, the situation was desperate. U.S., U. N. and South Korean forces were barely holding on to a small perimeter around the city of Pusan on the southern tip of Korea. General McArthur devised a plan to land Marines hundreds of miles north, behind the Communist lines, at Inchon on the Yellow Sea. This plan was unknown to any of us as we crossed the Pacific heading for Korea.

September 14, 1950. Our staff opened the Top-Secret Operations plan from General McArthur. We found we would attack Inchon, Korea, commencing at 0500 the next day. Our task force of four Navy aircraft carriers would be flying missions to support the thousands of Marines in amphibious ships as they assaulted the beaches at dawn, September 15, 1950.

The plan called for extensive Naval gunfire support. As one of two trained Naval gunfire spotters in Air Group Two, I would be flying this type of mission. Ironically, my main concern was that I had never led a mission from a ship, far at sea and returned. Being very junior, I had always flown on someone else's wing. Adding to my worries was the carrier electronic navigation homing device, "YG/ZB," of WWII vintage. The homer used code and I was lousy reading code. This homer required the pilot listen to a coded, low-frequency signal, sent out in 15-degree sectors around the ship. We had to note and record the code before we took off, and then follow the correct heading back to the ship. I had practiced this ashore, but never on the ship. I had trouble sleeping that night.

First Strikes

I was disappointed, I was not scheduled to fly on the first day of the Inchon invasion, September 15, 1950. I watched the takeoffs and landings of my buddies, then listened to their stories upon return. Our Air Group's Corsairs and Skyraiders supported the Marine assault troops, strafing and bombing, during the landing at Inchon. The assault was an

CHAPTER 1   FIRST COMBAT

overwhelming success. The landing achieved complete surprise, cutting the North Korean army's supply lines.

The next day, September 16, 1950, I was scheduled for two combat missions. On the first mission, I was scheduled as wingman for our Executive Officer, Lieutenant Commander Matthews. I was in a high state of excitement during the briefing, and manning. My Corsair was located deep in the "pack' of other Corsairs aft on the flight deck. I was thankful I was not one of the first row of Corsairs which had to be catapulted. I had never been catapulted, that thrill was reserved for a later date. However, only a foot separated

Catapulting Corsairs   Bill Crouse Photo

my propeller from the Corsair in front of me On starting, the wind blast and noise were terrifying. As the aircraft ahead of me added power to launch I was buffeted by their slipstream which threatened to push me into the aircraft behind me. Finally, it was my turn. I was taxied forward, spread and locked my wings, went over my check list. This launch was a deck run of 550 feet. It was a bight, clear day. I concentrated on joining-up and flying a smart right wing on LCDR Matthews, keeping my eyes open and my mouth shut.

Our four Corsairs were each loaded with eight HVAR 5-inch rockets. We proceeded to Inchon hitting railroads and

CHAPTER 1 FIRST COMBAT

targets of opportunity. During this mission, I just hung tight on Lieutenant Commander Matthew's right wing and shot when he shot, or rocketed when he rocketed, as a good wingman should. I saw no enemy fire and very few good targets. I was disappointed. We returned to the ship orbiting, waiting our turn to land. Combat was not what I expected.

Later that day, I was scheduled to lead a two-aircraft section, spotting gunfire for a gun cruiser at Inchon. Ensign Loomer was assigned as my wingman. My main concern was navigation, finding the ship upon our return. Again I manned aircraft aft on the flight deck in what we called the "Pack." Our aircraft were buried deep among many other Corsairs with wings folded, near the stern. Manning, starting, and taxiing out of the Pack remained very intimidating to me. On the signal to "start aircraft," there were dozens of barking engines, whirling propellers and smoke in front, in back and on both sides, just a foot or two away. I was terrified. Would I slide into the aircraft ahead? I locked my feet on the brakes while the wind and "prop-wash" buffeted me.

ENS Jim Brogan Sept 16, 1950

Tough crewmen crouching by each of my front main mounts grasped the heavy wooden chocks holding my wheels in the whirlwind blasts from the aircraft launching ahead. The flight deck turned into a virtual hurricane, a maelstrom of wind blasting down the deck, viciously buffeting aircraft and crewmen in the Pack as each aircraft went to full power.

Suddenly, black smoke poured down the deck, the ship turned sharply to starboard heeling steeply to port. Off to my left,

CHAPTER 1   FIRST COMBAT

on the water, appeared a patch of burning fuel with a helmetless pilot in the middle, splashing the flames away from himself. As the pilot came abeam of me, I could tell from his profile that it was Ensign Jim "Rube" Brogan, my bunkroom roommate. I keyed the mike and said, to no one in particular, "Brogan."

My heart raced as I went through my checks. I quickly prepared for the moment when the yellow-shirted director pointed to me and gave the signal, "Pull chocks," his thumbs pointing outward. With this signal, my plane captain quickly slid his chocks from my wheels, staying low and away from my big prop until he was safely in the catwalk. I added power to come forward out of the Pack, spread and locked my wings, put down my flaps, put the mixture "rich," and the prop "low pitch."

I was now in position to launch. The Launching Officer in yellow, "Fly One," pointed his flag at me with a rotating motion, asking for full power.

As he pointed down the deck, toward the bow, my left hand pushed the throttle to the firewall. My big Pratt Whitney engine roared its 2,250 horsepower. I accelerated rapidly past the flags snapping above the bridge, angling down the deck toward the starboard bow.

I was airborne! I made my clearing turn to the right, gear up, canopy closed, flaps up, heading for the rendezvous over the ship, setting up an orbit. In a half of a turn, Ensign Loomer, my wingman, joined and I set a course to the east. I broke out my maps, heading for Inchon Harbor.

Launch Em Bill Crouse Photo

I started to relax. It was a beautiful day, bright and clear. Checking in on the assigned frequency with

CHAPTER 1   FIRST COMBAT

the USS Mount McKinley, the amphibious command ship, I was assigned to the heavy cruiser, USS Rochester CA-124, for shore bombardment. The Rochester sent me to an area in Inchon City, instructing me to select targets of opportunity.

Dropping down below a thousand feet, I began searching for likely targets such as guns, tanks or troops. It was a heavily populated area with many people in the streets. People were waving flags. I dropped down low enough to get a good look at the flags, something I wouldn't do after I gained some experience with ground fire. They were waving Japanese flags!

I knew enough of history to know the Koreans had been under Japanese rule prior to World War II. I guessed these Japanese flags were the only flags they had. I assumed they were friendly.

I could find no tanks or troops. I told the USS Rochester that it would be unwise to fire into this area because there were many innocent people. The Rochester insisted that I find a target. They wanted to shoot! I searched and searched, but could find no guns, troops, trains or any obvious military targets in that area. Finally, in disgust, they released me.

Loomer and I were both armed with eight 5-inch rockets, so I flew towards the capital, Seoul, beyond the range of the

VF–64 Corsairs in route to the target Sept 1950 - Jimmy Dick

Chapter 1   First Combat

Rochester's guns. I found a rail yard with many North Korean railroad cars.

Now, this was more like it. I launched my high velocity aircraft rockets (HVAR) in pairs. The HVARs tore off my wings with the satisfying roar of a freight train. The rockets exploded in blasts of fire and flames throwing rail cars from the tracks leaving them torn and burning. We made repeated runs blasting many cars from the tracks then strafed with our 50 calibers, setting more cars afire.

After expending our ordnance came my big test. I turned out to sea and headed west for the USS Boxer. I tuned in the YG/ZB to listen. At first I heard nothing. I continued on my course flying west, out into the seemingly endless Yellow Sea.

Loomer disappeared from my wing. I turned and craned my neck, but could not see him. I called him, no answer. Suddenly, he zoomed from under my nose going straight up. He was playing games. I told him, "Damn it Loomer. Join up and stop screwing around!" I was on edge and worried I would not find the ship.

I kept a dead-reckoning plot on my plotting board. It showed we should be within fifty miles of the USS Boxer. There was nothing, just the endless Yellow Sea as far as I could see. I continued. When I estimated I was still 25 miles from the ship, I started to pick up a broken code. Soon, I was receiving the correct code for the 270 sector. I continued on the west heading as the signal continued to build. At about 10 miles, I began to see the task force, four carriers surrounded by a ring of destroyers. Relief!

Now my task was to pick out the USS Boxer from the four aircraft carriers, three were of the same class, and one a light carrier. Boxer's hull number, 21, was painted on the flight deck. I easily selected it from the USS Valley Forge, number 45, and USS Philippine Sea, number 47. Before launching, we were assigned a holding altitude over the ship, so I proceeded to that altitude, joining other VF-24 Corsairs orbiting the ship. Our squadron skipper was the junior skipper, so our squadron's landing order was last.

Chapter 1 First Combat

Orbiting overhead the USS Boxer, waiting for aircraft in the pattern ahead of us to land, I had a chance to look around. I was astounded to see dozens of gigantic Portuguese Men of War jelly fish, just below the water surface. They were so large, at first I thought they were mines. They were multi-colored, greens, reds and yellow, with long tentacles. When the ship sailed through a pack of these monsters, they were torn apart by the screws, leaving pieces trailing in the wake. I dreaded the thought of going into that water.

It seemed to take forever for the aircraft ahead of me to get aboard. There were several flight deck crashes. Finally, the lower circle cleared out, and I led Ensign Loomer up the starboard side of the Boxer at 250 feet. I broke to get my interval on a Corsair in front of me, downwind. I put my gear down, flaps down, hook down. I came aboard in order, with no problems.

I had led my first combat mission. The gun fire spotting mission was a bust, but I had made a good decision refusing to bombard innocent civilians and we did a good job with our rockets against the trains. My confidence was growing.

I visited Jim Brogan in sick bay that evening. He was burned on his face and neck. He was in some pain, but in good spirits. He said his engine lost power on take off, his 150 gallon belly-tank blew up when his Corsair hit the water. He was lucky to live through it. I told him I saw him go by in a

VC-3 F4U-5 Landing, USS Boxer, September 1950

Chapter 1   First Combat   9

patch of fire, splashing the flames away from himself, as we had been taught in training. He said, "How did you know it was me?" I said, "Your ears Rube, your ears." We had a laugh at that. He had distinctive ears.

No Kudos

In general, our novice Air Group had big problems. We were slow launching and recovering aircraft.

The Task Force Commander sent us a message that said, "To Boxer/Air Group Two: Your launch and recovery was one of the poorest I have witnessed in my 30 years of Naval Aviation experience."

We were mostly green Ensigns, just out of flight training. We had much to learn about fleet operations. It would have to be on-the-job training.

The three large aircraft carriers in our task force, USS Valley Forge, USS Philippine Sea and USS Boxer, commenced flying maximum combat strikes each day. The Marines fought hard toward Seoul. It was our to job to provide close air support directly to the front-line troops, as well as provide gunfire spotting for Naval ships, bomb and strafe enemy trains, trucks and any other military targets we found.

Air Group Two made progress toward being a more effective fighting force, but we were paying a price. We found that the enemy had effective anti-aircraft guns and they were very capable gunners. I first learned this lesson on September 19, flying my fourth combat mission.

First Flak

On September 19, 1950. I was scheduled to lead a Naval gunfire spotting mission. I had quickly overcome my trepidation about finding the carrier. I had flown several gunfire spotting missions for destroyers, cruisers and battleships. Our gunfire spot missions the aircraft were always loaded with rockets, bombs and machine gun ammunition, just as the strike aircraft. After completing my

CHAPTER 1   FIRST COMBAT   10

Plane Captain walks Corsair forward

gunfire spotting missions, I always conducted my own two-plane attack on targets of opportunity. It gave me great freedom of action, some of these missions were quite exciting and apparently I talked too much about them with other squadron pilots. I speculated that my commanding officer, LCDR Coffman, had overheard this talk, and requested to fly with me to check it out. Now, commanding officers don't usually fly on an Ensign's wing. I couldn't sleep well that night.

At the briefing, I said, "I assume, Sir, you will lead this mission?" He replied, "No, you lead it." I was petrified. My commanding officer was going to fly my wing.

I briefed the mission, we manned aircraft, launched and proceeded to the beach. I made landfall at Inchon as planned, I checked-in with the control ship, USS Mount McKinley, and asked for my gunfire spotting assignment. They informed me that there would be no gunfire spotting that day, the Marines had already advanced beyond Naval gunfire range. However, they requested, "Find the condition

################################

THAT I MIGHT ACHIEVE........
GHT LEARN HUMBLY TO OBEY....
 MIGHT DO GREATER THINGS....
 I MIGHT DO BETTER THINGS.
 MIGHT BE HAPPY..............
I MIGHT BE WISE..............
MIGHT HAVE THE PRAISE OF MEN,
 I MIGHT FEEL THE NEED OF GOD.
AT I MIGHT ENJOY LIFE.........
IGHT ENJOY ALL THINGS.
 FOR, BUT EVERYTHING I HAD HOPED FOR.
UNSPOKEN PRAYERS WERE ANSWERED....
ICHLY BLESSED!

####################################

############################

I ASKED GOD FOR STRENGTH,
I WAS MADE WEAK, THAT I MI
I ASKED FOR HEALTH, THAT I
I WAS GIVEN INFIRMITY THAT
I ASKED FOR RICHES, THAT I
I WAS GIVEN POVERTY, THAT
I ASKED FOR POWER, THAT I
I WAS GIVEN WEAKNESS, THAT
I ASKED FOR ALL THINGS, TH
I WAS GIVEN LIFE, THAT I M
I GOT NOTHING THAT I ASKED
ALMOST DESPITE MYSELF, MY
I AM AMONG ALL MEN, MOST F

############################

Chapter 1   First Combat

of the rail line running northeast from Inchon to Seoul. Is it intact or is it destroyed?"

From Inchon, I found the rail lines, dropped down to 1,000 feet then turned northeast weaving back and forth over the rail line, to determine its condition. The Skipper stayed about 1,000 feet in trail behind me. The rail line was a double-track rail line. I noticed that even though it had been bombed in many places, the North Koreans had repaired the tracks in such a way that at least one line was still open. I could see one line was shiny, glinting in the sun. They had been running trains. I relayed this information to the USS Mount McKinley.

I continued north at about 1,000 feet and 180 knots, slowly weaving back and forth and reporting back to the USS Mount McKinley. About 10 miles northeast of Inchon, I could see the rail lines crossing the Han River on multiple bridges.

Suddenly, a volley of fat red balls of fire rose slowly then raced towards my windscreen. "Flak!" The very first volley looked like it was going to hit me between the eyes. It almost did. I instinctively ducked. The rounds passed just inches over my head and hit my vertical stabilizer slicing off the top of my rudder.

I was enveloped in heavy streams of 40MM tracers and bursting flak.

Lieutenant Jimmy Dick VF-64, belly tank and bombs

Chapter 1   First Combat

Ensign Dave Leue' September 19, 1950 USS Boxer

I instinctively pushed my throttle to the firewall and maneuvered violently, "jinking" my way out of the flak. I picked up speed rapidly. The Skipper called me, "Slow down, Dave, slow down. Your rudder is coming apart!"

The Skipper joined on my right wing. He asked me if I wanted to land at Kimpo Airfield in Seoul, which the Marines had recently captured. I replied, "I'd like to see how my Corsair handles at landing speeds, then decide." I knew I would have to jump if I couldn't control my plane at landing speeds. I slowed the Corsair down, flying south towards Inchon. I opened the canopy, put down my flaps, and

Chapter 1   First Combat

LSO Zettle holds a "Roger"

checked out the slow flight characteristics of my damaged aircraft.

I slowed to 87-90 knots. It flew okay. I told the Skipper I would prefer to return to the ship, which we did. I made a wide gentle approach getting a "cut" on the first pass. In the ready room, Lt Zettle, our LSO, gave me an excellent grade for my landing. I felt good.

I learned a valuable lesson. I was fortunate to live through it. In the future, I made it an axiom: Don't get caught low and slow in areas such as bridges, where there could be a high concentration of flak.

The Learning Curve

Our four carriers in the task force hammered the North Koreans daily. Each carrier was launching twenty to forty aircraft, every three hours. We were hitting bridges, fuel dumps, trains, trucks, barracks and North Korean troops. Cruisers and battleships used their naval guns to disrupt trains and other targets near the coast. Air Group Two began to look more like a well-trained air group. The few North Korean fighter aircraft were all destroyed in the first days of the war. The Korean Army was rapidly disintegrating. We had cut their supply lines. The U.S. Marines, Army and U.N. troops were all advancing to the north.

Our main threats were the inherent risks in carrier operations and the heavy anti-aircraft fire from constantly moving, rapid-fire weapons made in Russia and China. The North Korean gun crews got plenty of practice as Navy Corsairs and Skyraiders dove through their fields of fire hundreds of times a day.

Chapter 1 First Combat

My Pilot's Log Book

I made brief notes in my Pilot's Log Book of our operations, the aircraft we lost, shot down or damaged by accidents:

September 16, 1950, Lieutenant Commander Taylor, VA-65, shot down near Inchon. KIA.

September 16, Lieutenant Commander Leonard Robinson, VF-63 Shot down Inchon, rescued.

September 16, Ensign Jim Brogan, lost power on takeoff, crashed at sea, rescued, burned, will recover.

September 19, Ensign Leue', hit by 40mm north of Seoul, recovered Boxer.

September 20, Lieutenant Junior Grade Smith, VF -64, torque rolled over the side on late wave off, lost at sea.

September 20, Lieutenant Junior Grade Seeman, VA-65, shot down in flames over Seoul. KIA.

September 23, Ensign Hitchcock, VA-65, hit by flak, landed Kimpo.

September 26, Ensign Bass, VF-63, spun in at the Ninety, got out OK.

September 29, Ensign Howell, VF-24, shot down 8 mi. north of Seoul, bailed out OK, last seen heading for the hills, behind enemy lines. PS. found October 2nd by advancing US Marines, body still warm, shot in the back.

October 1, Ensign Smiley Doris, VF-63, shot down south of Pyongyang, (Ensign Bustard, flying Rescap, gave last 'smart-ass,' instructions to Smiley, "Don't get Laid, Smiley!") He didn't…..rescued by helicopter.

October 13, Ensign Haggarty, VF-64, spun in at the 90, rescued by helicopter.

A Life Change

Many of my good Navy friends were Catholic. Ned Steiner, my very best friend, had died tragically in flight training. Jim Brogan, Jimmie Parce, both Catholics, become my roommates on Boxer. They didn't preach, but I could see

CHAPTER 1   FIRST COMBAT

their strong moral values and spirituality. Jane Febrey and I had been engaged for almost three years. She was Catholic but never pressured me to become Catholic. In fact, it was assumed that we would marry as Catholic (her) and Protestant (me), like her stepmother and father. I had been taught most of the real or imagined ills of the Catholic Church by my mother and Protestant friends. However I was drawn to the Catholic Church by the strong example of my Catholic friends.

Early in flight training, when I started to lose friends due to accidents, I knew if I were to function effectively, I needed to be ready to die. I needed a deep faith.

On the trip across the Pacific to Korea, I had started to take religious instructions from Father Kusick, the USS Boxer's Catholic Chaplain. Jimmie Parce was my mentor, teaching me more about the Catholic Christian faith. Once in combat, early each morning before our missions, I began to go to Mass on a regular basis with Jim Brogan. He and I were both engaged to Catholic girls. Jim was a strong, steady, modest and moral young man. I greatly admired him.

Father Kusick heard of my being badly shot up during the gunfire spotting mission with the Skipper. He called me in and asked, "Well, Dave, are you ready to become a Catholic?" I said, "I'm ready." I made my first confession, I went to Mass and I made my first communion. I felt great. This was a significant decision that shaped the remainder of my life.

General MacArthur's Success, USS Boxer's Casualty

During September and October 1950, Air Group Two became a tough and effective fighting force. General McArthur's strategy of an amphibious landing behind North Korean lines at Inchon, backed by four Navy aircraft carriers, the U. S. Marines, Army, Air Force and U.N. forces, had totally routed the North Korean army.

General MacArthur's decision to chase the remnants of the North Korean army across the 38th parallel to unify Korea, was controversial. Nevertheless, U.S. and United Nations forces pushed north toward the Yalu River with the North Koreans in total disarray.

In October 1950, USS Boxer sustained a casualty to one of

CHAPTER 1   FIRST COMBAT   16

her four main reduction gears, which turned one of her four propellers. We operated briefly on three screws.

I flew my last combat mission on October 15th, a strike on Pukchong in Northeast Korea. Shortly thereafter, we were ordered back to the United States.

Going Home

This was great news. We headed for Alameda, California, on three screws, happy to be out of combat and on our way back to the good old USA. The Boxer arrived back in Alameda in early November 1950. Best of all, Jane and I could finally be married. We quickly began planning a December wedding.

I thought this would be the end of my combat.

It was just the beginning.

Chapter Two

Navy V-5 College Program

Background

Spring 1945. The allies were surging toward victory in WW II. War in Korea was nowhere on the horizon. Not one pundit nor one politician predicted it.

Here are the events that led me into that war.

This was my junior year in Buffalo Technical High School. Tech was located in a friendly, predominately black neighborhood in down-town Buffalo, New York. I commuted by trolley and bus from the east side of town where I lived with my mother and my older sister Dolly, in an upper flat. My father had died when I was twelve.

My mother worked at Bell Aircraft building P-63 fighters, all with red stars on their wings, bound for Russia. World War II, which had started in Europe in 1939, was raging. It was the major background event of my teenage years. Since 1941, our country had sustained hundreds of thousands of battle deaths and millions of wounded. Newspapers, radio and movies, the media of that day, were 100% supportive of our leaders and the military. The most popular songs, such as "The Boogie-Woogie Bugle Boy of Company B" or "American Patrol," were patriotic and upbeat. Bad news, such as the recent Battle of the Bulge, simply was not printed or discussed. No pictures or stories of dead or wounded American or Allied soldiers were allowed. We were only told about our victories. Young men, like myself, were eager to get into the fight. I was seventeen and would soon be classified "1A, Fit for Service," in the Draft.

I followed the news closely, and was fascinated by the war. I read and studied everything about fighter planes, bombers, tanks, weapons and the ongoing battles. I built model

Chapter 2 Navy V-5 College Program

Buffalo Evening News, May 7, 1945

airplanes, including the Russian "Stormovick." Of all our allies, the media glorified the Russians the most. Never mentioned by the press and unknown to me, were Joseph Stalin's killing of millions of his own people in the 1930s or the uncomfortable fact that Stalin started the war as an ally of Hitler. President Franklin D. Roosevelt and our press treated Stalin as a great man.

Victory in Europe came on May 7, 1945, when the Nazis surrendered. Celebrations were muted because everyone knew our biggest battle, for Japan, was yet to come. Battle-tested troops were being transported from Europe to the Far East, where they would join millions of freshly trained soldiers, sailors and Marines, for the horrendous invasion of the Japanese home islands. Based on recent Japanese military performance, everyone knew this would be a terrible fight. The battle for Okinawa was a foretaste of what was to come. In this battle, the Japanese were fighting our Army and Marines troops to the last man. They were unleashing thousands of Kamikaze (suicide) bombers on our fleet.

NY Times, September 2, 1945

In late August 1945, the country was electrified by the Atomic bombing of the Japanese homeland. Hiroshima was hit on August 6 and Nagasaki on August 9, 1945. Hundreds of thousands of Japanese citizens, non-combatants, were obliterated in the blink of an eye. This seemed to bother no one at the time.

Chapter 2   Navy V-5 College Program

They started it... we finished it. On September 2, 1945, the Japanese formally surrendered.

Total euphoria swept the country. In Buffalo, the streets were packed with citizens of all ages, dancing, hugging, kissing, laughing and smiling. I knew this was a day I would never experience again.

I began my senior year at Buffalo Technical High School with great optimism. There would never be another war, the future looked bright. Only we had the atomic bomb. The Russians were our best friends.

1946 - A Prayer Answered, The Navy V-5 Program

In life, following every extraordinarily euphoric moment, there follows a predictable downturn. January 1946, I had the "blues." I was standing in front of the local hangout, Deery's Drugstore, on the corner of Virgil Avenue down the street from our flat. Snow was falling. The GIs were all coming home and going to college on the GI Bill. We had no money for college. I was going nowhere.

Standing next to me in the falling snow was a fellow Buffalo Technical HS student. He was very excited and said, "I'm going to be a Naval Aviator! They're going to send me to college. It's a great program, I can't believe it, I made it into the Navy V-5 program!" I said, "What in the world is the V-5 Program and how can I get into it?" He said, "It's the Navy college and flight training program. If you are selected, they send you to two years of college, then you go to flight training. After flight training you are commissioned an Ensign, later you get to finish your degree. It's really a four-year, everything-paid scholarship. It's very, very hard to get in to. Only the very best can make it."

"Don't even try, you'll never make it," my friend said.

I had to try. I went home and told my mother about the program. The next day, we went together to the Navy recruiters in the Post Office in downtown Buffalo. There I took the local Navy test for the V-5 Program and passed it. A few days later, a TR, or Transportation Request, arrived in

Chapter 2   Navy V-5 College Program

Dave and Mother, 1946

the mail. This was my ticket to the Navy Regional Offices in Pittsburgh, Pennsylvania, where I would take three days of intensive tests for the Navy V-5 program. I took the train to Pittsburgh with eleven other hopeful high school seniors from Buffalo. The trip took about a half a day. We were lodged at the Pittsburgh YMCA and were given meal tickets for the Dinner Bell Restaurant. Before going to sleep that night in the YMCA, I prayed to God to please help me do well. I promised to clean up my act in the future.

The first day was devoted to batteries of written psychological tests and interviews. The second day was devoted to aviation aptitude tests. These included questions of direct aviation knowledge, as well as demonstrations on various devices to test our coordination, mechanical, aviation skills and aviation aptitude. The third day was a very comprehensive physical, including eyes, and a final interview.

Of the eleven men from Buffalo who went with me to Pittsburgh, three of us were accepted. I was sworn in as an Apprentice Seaman, US Naval Reserve. Coming home on the train, I was in seventh heaven. I was sure there would never be another war. My plan was to get an education, learn to fly, do my duty, get out and become an airline pilot.

The Navy V-5 program allowed me to attend any university that had a Naval Reserve Training Corps (NROTC) unit. I wanted to return to my roots in California. I planned to buy a Harley-Davidson motorcycle, then ride it to the College of the Pacific in Stockton, California. Unfortunately, I had no driver's license and we had no car in which to learn to drive. My friend's father, Bill Watson, volunteered to teach me to

Chapter 2 Navy V-5 College Program

drive in his 1936 Dodge. I was in such a hurry to get this done that I succeeded in miserably failing my driving test.

After this disappointing test, I concluded that enrolling in the University of Buffalo for the fall semester 1946 was the logical choice. I needed to get a job to help cover my expenses while going to school. The Navy was only going to pay my books, tuition and $50.00 per month. I first got a job in the office at the Standard Buffalo Foundry. I was assigned to the office adding figures and did not last long in the job. Mother assisted me in getting another job where she worked, at Buffalo Electro Chemical in Niagara Falls. This was a company that manufactured high test hydrogen peroxide for use in such things as missiles and submarines. The company was run by first-generation Germans, who had very heavy accents. My mother was fluent in German, so she fit right in. I was hired as a common laborer. My boss's name was Hummel. The hydrogen peroxide was made in large ceramic vats. Each vat had carbon and platinum "anodes" charged with direct current supplied by large overhead copper bus bars. My job, wearing a full rubber suit, was to periodically clean out the vats, take out the anodes then remove the blue yarn (asbestos) and platinum wire. This job lasted all summer.

The University of Buffalo

I enrolled in the University of Buffalo in the summer of 1946. I checked in at the Navy NROTC at the University of Buffalo, filled out the required forms, received directions to register for classes, then acquainted myself with the campus. There were no dorms. All students had to find their own lodging somewhere in town. I enrolled in engineering classes. My objective was a degree in mechanical engineering.

The University of Buffalo sat on a small hill surrounded by a vast green lawn and elm trees. The buildings style were classic old Gothic. It was a pleasant and inviting campus. It was not a large campus. The student body, I'm sure, was somewhat less than 3,000 students. The campus had a good

CHAPTER 2   NAVY V-5 COLLEGE PROGRAM   22

warm inviting feeling. I felt better about not going to California.

New Friends, Springville Avenue

The first semester I lived at home at 80 Virgil Avenue. This was not satisfactory, I lived too far from the campus. Halfway through the semester I went to the housing office at the University of Buffalo with Jim Carr, another Navy V-5 Apprentice Seaman I had met in class. Jim had rented a room near the campus, but was dissatisfied with his arrangements.

Jim Carr, Joe Zawotoski

Dave Leue', Gordon Sales

The housing office gave us several addresses to check out. The first place we looked at was an upper flat, just down the hill, two blocks from the University on Springville Avenue. Jim and I went together to inquire. We found that the landlords, a family named Alf, lived in the downstairs flat. They were already renting the upper flat to three World War II vets, who were also University of Buffalo students. We met the three vets, Joe Zawotoski, a former Army 2nd Lieutenant Combat Infantryman; Gordon Sales, a former Army Medic; and Vince LaRusso, a former Air Force enlisted man. We were accepted as roommates and moved in. This group of young men became my best friends.

We did all of our own shopping, cooking, dishwashing, clothes washing and housekeeping. For the most part, this went very well. Joe, Gordon, and Vince had already set up a routine, where they made out the dinner menus for a week, went shopping, then each would take a night to cook, another would cleanup, etc.

Jim and I fit nicely into this routine. Now there were five of us, one for each school day of the week. We bought a pressure cooker, which we used several times a week, to make meat and potatoes or stew. This device has mostly disappeared from the modern scene, but it was a godsend to us. Since it was a pressure device, it cooked in a fraction of the time of just heating or boiling on an open stove. Microwaves had not been invented. Generally, we would only cook on Monday, Tuesday, Wednesday and Thursday nights. Our breakfasts and lunches on Fridays and weekends were on our own. On weekends, Gordon went home to eastern New York and Jim went home to Red House, New York, about sixty miles south.

We set up our drawing boards for drafting. Each of us had a place to study. It was a good environment. Nobody drank and only occasionally did we have enough money to go out to eat. Joe, Gordon and Vince became my surrogate fathers. They were four or five years older than Jim and I, but all had much more life experience. They had fought and traveled the world in World War II. Joe Zawotoski, especially, became my mentor. I was too young and self centered to really understand the hell he'd been through as a combat infantryman in World War II. It took my own future combat experience to gain that understanding.

Jane Febrey

Two or three doors up the hill from where we lived on Springville Avenue lived a beautiful seventeen-year-old young lady. I noticed her as I walked up and down the street to and from school. I said, "hello" and we passed small talk on several occasions. She was usually helping around the house in some way, with an apron on or sweeping the porch. I found she was a junior at nearby Amherst High School and planned to become a nurse. Her name was Jane Febrey.

Chapter 2   Navy V-5 College Program

Jane Febrey, 1947

The rules of the day were you had to meet the girl's mother and father and be approved before you could take her out. A good old-fashioned rule. One evening, Jane invited me in to meet her father. Arnold was snoozing in his easy chair in the living room after dinner.

As time went by I was approved and I invited Jane to a movie. We started to date. In the process, I met her stepmother and sisters. Her stepmother, Vera, had married Arnold, her father, fifteen years earlier, after Jane's birth-mother died giving birth to Jane's sister, Ann. Vera was considerably younger than Arnold. Jane's youngest sister, Judy, Vera's only child, was about eight or nine years old, her sister Ann was fourteen.

Vera was an excellent hairdresser. She kept a small hairdresser's shop in the front of their lower flat. Arnold was the office manager for RKO, the movie distributor, in Buffalo. When we started to date, Arnold would get passes for Jane and me to the latest movies.

Jane was raised Catholic by her father; Vera was Protestant. Jane and her sisters went to Catholic grammar school through eighth grade, then went to public high schools.

Through the years, Arnold and I became very good friends and fishing buddies. He had a kindly face, a ready wit, was balding and in his forties. As Jane and I began to go steady, there was obvious concern from her parents because she was very young. In fact, we both were very young, I was a freshman college student and Jane was still a junior in high school. On occasion Vera would cook for me when it was my night to feed the boys in our flat. She usually prepared a wonderful casserole and salad.

Chapter 2 Navy V-5 College Program

Vera was attractive and vivacious and she became very popular with my four buddies. They loved it when she would cook for us. However, Vera was very realistic. I know she and Arnold worried about Jane and my relationship. In subtle ways, they tried to discourage us. We were kept under close observation. I also received advice from my buddies, including Vince, who frequently talked to Vera. He would subtly bring up Jane and caution me about becoming too serious with Jane. I could tell his arguments came from Vera.

Our romance persisted and towards the end of the year 1947, we decided to become engaged. By this time, Jane was attending the University of Buffalo in the Millard Fillmore Hospital nursing program. Our plan was that she would finish her nursing program, as she promised her parents, and I would complete my flight training and be commissioned. Then we would be married. This would take at least two years. (Actually, it would take four years.)

We knew this was going to be a difficult plan to carry out. We would be apart for extended periods of time. The risks were great. However we were certain of our path. I think Vera and Arnold went along with the plan sure that somewhere down the road, we would go our separate ways. In fact, Vera once said to me, "You'll find some blond in Pensacola, and we will never see you again." She said this half in jest, but I know she meant it. And if you looked at the situation from afar, the odds were really against us. But we had no doubt.

Ann, Vera, Judy, Jane Febrey

Chapter 2   Navy V-5 College Program   26

Joe Zawotoski

Joe Zawotoski 1947

Joe told me he was a Private in the Army stationed at Schofield Barracks on the Hawaiian Islands on December 7, 1941, when the Japanese attacked Pearl Harbor. Schofield Barracks was also a Japanese target that day. Joe, who would not talk much about his years of combat, nevertheless, told me a humorous story about that day. His buddies set up a 50-caliber machine gun and were shooting at the Japanese Zeros that were strafing their barracks. He said one of his buddies, in his exuberance, shot off the corner of their own barracks.

Joe went on from Pearl Harbor to land in North Africa in 1943. He was with General Patton when the U.S. invaded Sicily and he was with Patton again as the allies fought their way across Europe in 1944-45. He was severely wounded at Metz on the Siegfried Line in 1945. He finished the war as a First Lieutenant, a battlefield commission. You usually get a battlefield commission when everyone senior to you has been killed or wounded.

When I was eighteen, everything was going my way. I made a joke out of everything. I was doing this one day with Jim Carr. Joe, due to his war wound, was having trouble with his back. He tried to describe his wound. Something struck me funny. I started to laugh and Joe turned white. He thought I was making fun of him. I think he could have killed me on the spot, and probably should have. He didn't speak to me for a full two weeks.

Later, we were relaxing on a Sunday. I was reading Life Magazine. This was the famous issue of Life showing pictures of the frozen American GIs in the snow. These GIs had been machine-gunned at Malme'dy, Belgium, after

Chapter 2 Navy V-5 College Program

surrendering to LTCL Peiper's brigade, during the Battle of the Bulge. During the war, U.S. papers would not publish any photos of dead Americans, or for that matter, publish any material that was negative to the war effort. Here, a year or so after the war, I first saw these pictures, and I was shocked and enraged.

I started to swear, "Those lousy so-and-so Krauts." Joe was reading the paper on the other side of the room and said, "Dave, would you shut up!" I persisted, "Joe, look at what those SOBs did!!" He said, "So?" I said, "We would never do anything like that!" He said to me, "Dave, were you there?"

I was astonished. What he said, in so many words, was ... we did the very same thing! We never spoke of this again, or any of his war experiences. Joe Zawotoski had been through hell and back. There wasn't anybody that he could talk to about it, nobody, especially a dumb eighteen-year-old. It took me years to understand.

Later, Joe decided to change his name. He said, "I'm tired of a being treated like a dumb Pollock." By then, we had become very close fiends, I tried to dissuade him, telling him he should be proud to be Polish, they were great people and besides, he was an American, and who cared where you came from? He was adamant though, and he had his name changed to "Lane." Joe was a mixed up GI struggling to make sense of life after all he'd been through. I was too dumb and young to know what to do. To me, Joe was a giant and I will always hold him dearly in my heart.

Jim Carr

Jim Carr was a big happy-go-lucky red-headed farm boy, we called Red. We hit it off in the classes we took together and tried to help each other out. I was better at drafting and physics. He was better at math and calculus. Jim was from Red House, New York, about 60 miles south of Buffalo, in the Allegheny Mountains. In the 1940s, Red

Chapter 2 Navy V-5 College Program 28

Jim Carr 1947

House was still part of Allegheny State Park. His father, mother, brother and himself grew up on a small farm there.

In the winter of 1946, I was still living at 80 Virgil Avenue. Red invited me to come with him to his home in Red House, where we could ski and hunt deer. I readily accepted and we took the bus from Buffalo to Salamanca, near his home. I said to Red, "What happens if I kill a deer? How in the world will I bring it back?" He said, "Don't worry, I've never shot a deer in my life; the odds are very small you will." Deer were very scarce then.

The morning we went hunting his mother was up before dawn. She fixed us a fantastic breakfast with barley soup, chicken, eggs and bacon. She drove us to the woods in an area called the "Beauvais," dropped us off, wished us luck and said she would return in the late afternoon. She had given us an apple for lunch. We set off hunting together within about 100 or 200 yards apart. We had shotguns with rifled slugs, which were legal, but rifles were not. This area of the Allegheny Mountains was heavily forested. It was difficult to see more than 100 yards in any direction through the trees. At some point in the morning, we lost track of each other and I hunted most of the day by myself. I saw no deer. In the late afternoon I realized I'd better start back toward our starting point. I was moving fast through dry leaves, making a lot of racket, not really hunting. Suddenly, off to my left, a beautiful Whitetail buck ran by me, about 50 yards away. I quickly raised my shotgun and fired. The deer disappeared into the woods. I thought, "You dope, you missed him."

I ran through the woods in the direction he disappeared, hoping to get another shot. I came upon some spots of blood, which indicated I had hit him. I was taught, if you wounded a deer, you should sit down and wait, rather than run after him. The deer then, is more likely to lay down. It was very difficult for me, but I stopped and waited about five minutes, then took up the chase, running down the blood trail. I only ran for three or four minutes, when I almost ran over the deer. He had laid down, but now he jumped up in front of me. I shot him again and killed him. In all the years my father hunted, he had never killed a deer. This one was for him. He was a beautiful eight-point buck.

I gutted the deer. Then, using the rope I had brought, I dragged him back to the parking lot in the Beauvais. I sat down and waited for Jim. In about a half-hour I could hear him whistling down the hill. He came up to me and said, "Wow, you got a buck!" I said, "No, I'm just watching this deer for some guy. He'll be back soon." Previously, I had put my deer tag on the deer's antlers and Jim went over to look at the tag. When he saw the tag and read my name, he started laughing and we danced around and enjoyed the moment.

This one's for you, Dad

Jim's mother came and picked us up. We loaded the deer on the front fender, which you could do with cars in those days, and took it back to his farm. We hung the deer by the antlers from a tree in front of his house. We butchered it there; I gave half to his mother. I talked his uncle into taking me and the deer with him back to Buffalo. I took the head and antlers, wrapped in newspapers, on a trolley to the taxidermist, Mr. Huprick, in downtown Buffalo. I got so tied up in school and moving, it was six months before I went to pay for and pickup my deer head. Mr. Huprick was not pleased, he chewed me out. He had waited for six months for his cash. He did a beautiful job. I think it cost the extravagant sum of $35.

Chapter 2   Navy V-5 College Program   30

Gordon Sales

Gordon Sales was studying to be a doctor, taking pre-med classes. He was a slight fellow maybe 5-foot-9 or so, wore glasses, smoked a pipe, and had an intellectual air about him. He always wore his army fatigue jacket to and from class. Gordon was the quietest of our group, but he had a wry sense of humor. He made it clear that he wasn't about to take any guff from any eighteen year-olds, like Jim or me. I really admired his fatigue jacket and once he let me wear it. When I offered to buy the jacket from him he absolutely refused. In fact, he was indignant that I asked. I should've known that that jacket and he had gone through a lot together. He had been a combat medic in Europe, but he talked very little about his combat experience. He did tell me he had been in a reconnaissance battalion, which meant they were out in front of the main body of troops probing the enemy. Gordon had a German Lica reflex camera, which he confiscated from a wounded German officer they had captured. This German officer said to Gordon, "I know I'm out of the war now, please tell me about your automatic artillery." Gordon explained to me that we had no automatic artillery. What our gunners did was line up our batteries of 105 howitzers wheel to wheel, start the firing on one end of the line in sequence, and then keep it going. We had so many guns it just sounded automatic, especially if you were on the receiving end. He also told me that he very much appreciated our tactical Air Force at the time. Once his group entered a German town and there was a German Tiger tank at the other end of town, its turret pointing away from them. They called for air support and before the German tankers could turn their tank's gun on them, P-47 fighters dropped out of the sky and destroyed the Tiger tank. Although Gordon and I were never

Gordon Sales 1947

close, he was a good friend who always gave me wise counsel.

Joe's Prediction

We five college students lived noisily together in the upper flat, above the Alf's for more than a year. In general, we got along very well, with the exception of making too much noise during discussions and minor disagreements. Given the fact that those old houses had little insulation, we probably made too much noise on a regular basis. This came to a head on a Sunday afternoon.

This Sunday, we were discussing world events and our plans for the future. I told Joe I was going to be an airline pilot after I got out of the Navy.

Joe said to me. "Leue' you dumb bastard, if you make it through flight training, you are going to fight the Communists, mark my words!"

This was unbelievable to me. I became furious. I had been brought up on World War II propaganda. Stalin, the Communists, were our best friends. I invoked Roosevelt and Churchill. The argument quickly got out of hand and I went into a shouting stage. It was preposterous to me that we would ever fight our best friends.

Joe, Jim, Gordon

Joe Zawotoski, Second Lieutenant US Army, was honestly telling Dave Leue' what he had learned from Patton about the Communists. He was trying to tell me, honestly, what lay in my future. I wouldn't listen. I was eighteen and I knew everything.

The discussion got completely out of hand. I was standing on a chair yelling, shaking my fist at Joe. There was a "knock, knock, knock" on the door. Jim opened the door, it was Mr. Alf, our landlord. He said, "That's it, boys, you make much too much noise. You will have to find another place to stay." He gave us until the end of the semester to find another place.

I had gotten us thrown out!

Off to Pensacola

In the fall of 1947, we moved to a smaller flat at 44 Comstock Avenue. In the spring of 1948 upon completion of my college requirements, I received orders to report to Pensacola, Florida, to commence my flight training. Jim Carr did not receive his orders at that time, which was a disappointment. We had hoped to go to flight training together.

I left a few belongings and photographs in a trunk with the Febreys, said my goodbyes to family, friends and especially to Jane. I knew this was going to be hard on Jane. I was going to miss her, of course, but I was off on a great adventure, flight training and Naval Aviation. I had my fears, she was a beautiful young woman and I was going to leave her for months or years at a time. Nevertheless, we were both certain that this was what we wanted. We went forward with confidence. We promised to write every day, and for the most part, we kept that promise.

On the day I left, Jane had to be in class. My sister, Dolly, took me to the train. I boarded the train with about a dozen hopeful future naval aviators bound for Pensacola, Florida. It was definitely with mixed emotions that I left my beautiful sweetheart and set off to test myself against the world.

Chapter Three

Basic Training, Pensacola

Pensacola, Florida—Preflight

I boarded the train for Pensacola at the downtown Buffalo station in May 1948. There was a large group of V-5 Apprentice Seamen on the train. It was a two and half day trip to Pensacola, so we were accommodated in sleeping cars or Pullman's. This was my first experience with this luxury. I always traveled with my family in coach.

Harvey Graf, Dave, Paul Gilbert

Upon arriving in Pensacola we were picked up in Navy buses and taken into the NAS Pensacola base. We immediately went through the normal military routine for new recruits: haircuts, issuing uniforms, organizing into groups, then assignment to barracks.

The Preflight buildings were full. We were put up in old World War II barracks for two weeks before starting our regular Preflight classes. Chief Petty Officers indoctrinated us in military drill, discipline, Navy customs and care of our uniforms. We worked on the flight line doing what was called "Tarmac," fueling and cleaning of aircraft.

NAS Pensacola Preflight Barracks

When our time came to enter Preflight, we were

CHAPTER 3   BASIC TRAINING, PENSACOLA

assigned rooms in groups of six and organized in platoons of approximately twenty. We were sworn in as Midshipmen Fourth Class, United States Navy, "Plebes," the lowest rating, equivalent to first-year Midshipman at the Naval Academy.

Preflight Platoon

Kohler, Kowalski, Leue', Milway

Our platoon leader was a southern boy from Mobile, Alabama, Bill Lindsay. Bill had been to military school and was a good man to teach us and lead us. Preflight had several missions. The first was to indoctrinate us in military discipline, Navy customs and traditions. The second was to teach the basics of aviation, specifically naval aviation. Our classes covered aircraft engines, navigation, gunnery, aerodynamics, flight procedures, as well as purely military courses such as Essentials of the Naval Service, survival and physical training, lots of physical training. Intensive swimming, marching and survival instruction were interspersed with our academic classes. We also had classes in communication, which in those days included, "Code and Blinker." Code, Morris code, the "dits" and "dahs" and Blinker, long and short signals of light. Because of my propensity to mix up letters and numbers, I had a hard time with "Code & Blinker."

Most of my buddies had no problem with Code & Blinker, especially those who had a musical ear. I spent extra time at night studying until finally, I could pass the tests, but I was never very good at it. We had to be able to copy eight words a minute of code and four words a minute of blinker to pass. (It would be years before I understood I had dyslexia). In all other subjects, I excelled, especially engines and aerodynamics, most of which I had learned building and flying airplane models.

CHAPTER 3   BASIC TRAINING, PENSACOLA

Drill Sweat

The physical demands and the demands on our time were extreme. I started out skinny and lost weight as we progressed through the four months of training.

This was an all-volunteer program and even at this early stage, some of my buddies did not adapt well, and decided to go home.

The daily routine went something like this: up at 5 a.m., wash, dress and shave, go to your cleaning detail, swab down a group of passageways, fall in with your platoon at six, march to the mess hall, fallout and eat, fall in, march to your first class, after class, fall in, march to swimming, dress for swimming. After swimming, cleanup and dress, fall in, march to navigation, aerodynamics, engines, on through the day.

We had to change clothes three or four times a day, and I was always slow changing. We marched each day with rifles, learning the basics of drill. Our drill instructors were Marines, who professed no love for Navy types. They seemed to take diabolic delight imprinting their military skills on us. I knew that this type of harassment was part of military training and I took it in stride.

Extra Duty

After evening chow, we had time to study until 10 p.m., then it was lights out. At times, I wrote letters to Jane, after lights out, in the "Head." Once, I was put on report for this, by "Mighty Mouse," the infamous gym instructor. If you were put on report you usually were given, "Ten and Four" (Ten Demerits and four hours Extra Duty). Hours had to be "Walked off" with a rifle on the weekends. We only had Sundays off, so demerits were a big burden. Too many demerits and you were

CHAPTER 3   BASIC TRAINING, PENSACOLA

sent home. Despite a few bumps, I thrived and enjoyed the challenge of our rigorous training.

I was in "Batt Four," Battalion Four. To foster spirit, there were weekly competitions between battalions. Two of my five roommates, twins, Joe and John Richardson, were short, well-built and excellent boxers. They were in charge of the Battalion Four boxing team. They tried to recruit me. I told them I had no desire to box. Joe Richardson said, "Come on, Leue', we'll show you how, you'll do good!" Joe pointed out that everyone wore head protection and used big gloves.

He said, "Leue', you can't get hurt!" They persisted and finally, I said, "OK, I'll box in competition." They taught me the basics by light sparing in our time off. When the time came for the competition, I asked them to please get me an opponent that looked skinnier than I. We laughed as we looked across the ring at my opponent before the match, he looked like a pushover.

Well, he flattened me. I did get up off of the deck and made a good fight of it, but that was the end of my boxing career.

I excelled at swimming. I had no problem with the demanding swimming standards. We were taught how to jump from platforms, tie our trouser legs and inflate them as floatation aids, and how to swim through burning oil.

The final test required we swim a mile with our clothes on. Several of my buddies failed the tough swimming tests and were sent home.

Preflight Swim Class

My platoon leader, Bill Lindsay, and I became close friends. Toward the end of Preflight, when we were allowed weekends off, he invited me to his home in Mobile, Alabama. Among other things, we

Chapter 3 Basic Training, Pensacola

went to a football game at his old high school, I met several of his friends, his girlfriend, and his family. I gained a flavor of the old South and how families lived. (Bill Lindsay would be one of the first of us to die in an aircraft accident, shortly after joining the fleet in 1950.)

The four months of Preflight went by like the wind. We came out of Preflight with smart military bearing, trim and fit. We had learned the basic knowledge and skills necessary to begin flight training. We were becoming "Blue and Gold."

Whiting Field — "A" Stage, Safe for Solo

Whiting Field is located just to the northeast of Pensacola. It is a two airfield complex, North and South Whiting. I was assigned to South Whiting Field. The barracks were old World War II wooden barracks in a very sad state of repair. They reflected the tight post war military budgets, when Louis Johnson was Secretary of Defense, under President Harry Truman. However, we did not care, we were about to begin flying and would have been happy if they put us up in tents.

At Whiting Field, I first met Ned Steiner, who would become my best friend. He was a Catholic boy from Gary, Indiana. He was so full of life, at times he had trouble containing his enthusiasm. One evening, I was walking through our ratty barracks when, without warning, he knocked me down with a blast of water from a fire hose. Thus began a wild water fight with fire hoses. Luckily we cleaned up the mess before the Officer of the Day made his rounds.

We were assigned instructors to begin the first stage, "A" Stage, of flight training. We were promoted to Third Class Midshipmen, no longer Plebes. "A" Stage consisted of twenty flights leading to soloing. Our training aircraft were the North American SNJ. During World War II, the SNJ was an advanced trainer. It would now be our primary trainer. The SNJ had a 600-

Whiting Field Ready Plane

Chapter 3   Basic Training, Pensacola

horsepower radial engine, a tail wheel and was a lot of airplane to start out in. My first instructor's name was Lieutenant Barfield. He had been an F6F fighter pilot during World War II. In the SNJ, the student sat in the front seat, the instructor sat in the rear.

On my first flight, Lieutenant Barfield took the airplane off, then at altitude had me take the controls and try basic maneuvers. After an hour and a half of exploring the basic characteristics of the SNJ, Lieutenant Barfield took the controls and returned to South Whiting Field and landed the airplane.

On the next flight, I was required to taxi the airplane, then take off with assistance, raise the landing gear, then fly to the practice area. Hundreds of Navy airplanes were operating in the Pensacola airspace. A primary safety consideration during all of training was to see, and avoid, collisions with other aircraft.

We wore parachutes and were trained to bail out of the airplane in an emergency. In preflight, we had thoroughly studied the operation of the SNJ, its engine and controls. So, now we were in flight training we were expected to progress rapidly.

By the third flight, Lieutenant Barfield had me land the SNJ at an outlying grass field called "Pace." At altitude, I was then taught how to recognize a stall (the wing loses its lift), how to recover from a stall, how to spin (an auto-rotating stall) and recover from a spin.

By the fourth flight, I was introduced to "High" and "Low" altitude emergency procedures; what to do if the engine fails on take off and what to do if it fails at altitude. These

Bail Out Trainer South Whiting Field,

CHAPTER 3   BASIC TRAINING, PENSACOLA

emergency procedures were practiced on each flight thereafter. You could expect after each take off from a touch-and-go landing, the instructor would pull back the throttle and say, "Your engine has failed." You had to put the nose down immediately to keep flying speed, pick up the landing gear, put down the flaps and point the nose at the softest spot in sight. This was the "Low- altitude" emergency procedure. We were taught to never turn back to the field.

For a "High-altitude" emergency, the instructor would cut the throttle unexpectedly. I was expected to glide to a field and land the airplane. There were many grass fields that we used for this practice.

On my Number "10" check ride, I was assigned a check pilot, LT Myjock, who would rate my progress in take offs, stalls, spins, high-and-low-altitude emergencies and landings. If I was satisfactory, I would continue with my instructor. If not, I would be given extra time and then be required to fly two satisfactory check rides. If I was not successful in both, I would be washed out of the program and sent home or to the Fleet. The pressure was building. I could not imagine failure.

10 Check Ride

I passed my "10" check satisfactorily. Shortly thereafter, Lieutenant Barfield was transferred and I was given a new instructor, Lieutenant Myers. LT Myers was an old-time instructor and we got along wonderfully. He modified many techniques that Lieutenant Barfield had taught me. I felt very comfortable under his guidance.

Christmas Leave

We had been in Pensacola since May. At Christmas, we were granted ten days leave. Twenty-five or thirty Midshipmen from Buffalo got together to pool their resources. We chartered a DC-3 for a flight to and from Buffalo. The flight took most of a day coming and going, so we had about a week home. It was a wonderful time. I stayed with the Febreys on Springville Avenue. Jane and I danced, went to shows, visited family and friends, took a trip to Niagara Falls and just enjoyed being together. The time went too fast. I couldn't believe it when we had to return. I felt very good after this visit. Even though I had to leave Jane again, our plan was working and we were even more in love.

Buffalo 1948

My flight training progressed rapidly after Christmas. Before I knew it, I was scheduled for my final flight with my instructor, which was flight 18. On this flight, I was shooting touch-and-go landings at Pace field when LT Myers told me to land and pull up to a corner of the field.

I stopped the airplane. He climbed out with the engine running and said, "OK, Leue', you're on your own, show me a couple good landings."

I took off, made two landings, and taxied back to pick him up. We took off and flew back to South Whiting where LT Myers told me, "You are ready for your 'A' Stage check ride!"

On the "A" Stage check ride, I would be evaluated for "Safe for Solo" by a special Check Pilot. Each Check Pilot had a reputation, some for being easy, they were called "Santa Claus," and others as "Down Check." I drew a notorious Down Check pilot, LT Trammel.

Solo

I was very nervous before my "A" stage check ride. It was a cloudy, hazy day and I had trouble seeing the horizon well. We were taught to fly by nose attitude and, at that stage, the horizon was very important to me. I went through all the required maneuvers, a series of stalls, the low-altitude and high-altitude emergencies, then touch-and-go landings at Pace field. LT Trammel said nothing. Somehow, I felt the

CHAPTER 3   BASIC TRAINING, PENSACOLA   41

flight was not going well. As we headed back to South Whiting, he said to me, "OK, show me a nice landing." I figured I still had a chance for an "UP." I made what appeared to me to be a good landing.

We got out and he came up to me and said, "Very nice flight, you are safe for solo!"

I was stunned. This was a tremendous step for me. It was January 8, 1949.

Solo! January 8, 1949

Later that day I took off on my first solo into the gloriously sunny Pensacola sky in WB 434 for an hour of pure pleasure. It was hard to believe. The Navy trusted me with this fine aircraft. I didn't even have a driver's license.

"B" Stage— Mild Aerobatics

In "B" Stage, we flew one flight with our instructor, and then two solo flights, practicing the new maneuvers we were taught on the initial flight with our instructor. This stage was designed to build our skills, confidence and to learn mild aerobatic maneuvers. We continued to fly out of South Whiting Field. The new maneuvers introduced were called, "Wing-Overs" and "Chandelles."

A Wing Over is executed by pulling the aircraft nose up 45 degrees, while simultaneously rolling the wings into a 90-degree bank, then after 90 degrees of turn, gradually reducing your bank, while putting your nose back down 45 degrees, reversing direction 180 degrees, ending at the same altitude, the same airspeed, in the opposite direction.

A Chandelle is executed by slowly pulling the aircraft nose up 10 to 15 degrees, increasing bank to 45 degrees, turning 90 degrees, then decreasing the bank slowly until you've turned 180 degrees, while climbing, 1000 feet higher.

CHAPTER 3   BASIC TRAINING, PENSACOLA   42

On our solo flights we would practice these maneuvers, plus stalls and spins at altitude, then come down and shoot touch and go landings at an outlying field, then go back and land at Whiting Field. My confidence was quickly building. It had taken a dip during my first solo in "B" Stage, when I heard on the radio, "Send an ambulance to South Field, there has been a crash." I listened and realized that an instructor and student had spun in and were killed. I realized even aviators with great experience, such as instructors, could make a fatal mistake. One of my classmates landed, taxied his plane in, shut down the engine, and quit the program.

I realized that if I was to persist and flourish in Naval Aviation, I would need three things. Be a very good aviator, have a very strong faith and be ready to die. I prayed on a daily basis, many times a day.

"B" Stage consisted of twenty flights, and they went quickly. The January weather was perfect and I completed "B" Stage before the end of January. The "B" Stage check ride was much less stressful than the "A" Stage check ride. I easily passed. This meant that I would be going on to Corey field, a small field closer to Pensacola, where they taught aerobatics, "C" Stage. I packed my gear and headed for Corey field. I was also promoted to Second Class Midshipmen, two stripes on my Shoulder Boards. A big deal.

1949 Safety Poster

Corey Field "C" Stage—Aerobatics

The barracks at Corey field were in much better shape than those at Whiting. The field was small and it was located close to the main field at Pensacola. We had to be more careful in the traffic pattern, taking off and landing. We were mixed in with advanced students in Corsairs and other fleet aircraft. This flying was the most fun so far.

Chapter 3 Basic Training, Pensacola   43

My new instructor for Aerobatics was a World War II torpedo plane pilot, Lieutenant Anderle. He was very calm, cool and professional. Lieutenant Anderle would demonstrate an aerobatic maneuver or two; I would practice them with him, then I would have two solo flights to practice the new maneuvers. I learned loops, slow rolls, barrel rolls, wing over rolls, "Emmelman" turns and the "Split S."

This was really fun flying. The SNJ was just like a little fighter and it was just loads of fun to learn and practice these maneuvers. I naturally took to the "Gee" forces and being on my back. I loved it. We had to fly each maneuver in a very precise way. There were certain airspeeds and altitudes that you had to start and finish each maneuver. So, like ice skaters, we were judged on the precision of our maneuvers.

Dave, Corry Field

"C" Stage went rapidly with good weather. I completed it by the end of February 1949. This stage gave me great confidence. Aerobatic flying gave me a great sense of freedom and joy.

My log book shows that Lieutenant Pervis gave me my "C" Stage check ride. I had never flown with him before. I went through the whole repertoire of maneuvers and he said not one word. When I finished, he said, "That was very good, but may I show you a thing or two?" He then proceeded to fly all of the maneuvers, with a very smooth touch. He said, "Try that." I went through all of the maneuvers trying to mimic his technique. It was more pleasant for both of us and the airplane. Lieutenant Pervis started me on the road to being a smooth pilot.

CHAPTER 3   BASIC TRAINING, PENSACOLA

"D" Stage—Instruments

I was pleased that Lieutenant Anderle would be my instructor for "D" Stage-Instruments. Instruments were a brand-new experience, an unnatural skill to learn. We were given extensive lectures on the physiology of the body and how it influenced our perception of "up." It was explained that from the time we are born we perceive how to stay upright, unconsciously observing the horizon, through muscular clues and information from the semicircular canals in our ears, which act like little gyros.

Our natural system of orientation works well even if we are in a dark room with no lights, because we can feel the vertical through our body, and our semicircular canals give us a reference to the last time we saw the horizon.

As soon as we are in an airplane, however, this system breaks down if we can't see the horizon. If there are positive Gees on the body in a turn, then "down" feels like wherever the Gee is coming from, which might be from any direction, not the real down. The semicircular canals cannot detect very low rates of turn or roll. Thus, in a cloud, we quickly develop vertigo, that is, loss of the sense of where up or down is, and will lose control of the airplane. You cannot fly an airplane by the "seat of the pants," without instruments.

Lieutenant Anderle

This is relatively easy to understand, but difficult to learn, because our natural instincts are so powerful. Even knowing this, our natural instincts can overpower what our instruments tell us and give us vertigo. This is the challenge of learning and flying instruments.

Our instrument training began in the "Link" Trainer, the very first flight simulator. The Link Trainer, was designed before World War II by the genius, Mr. Edwin Link.

CHAPTER 3 BASIC TRAINING, PENSACOLA 45

Link Instrument Trainer

This trainer was a little blue box, with stubby wings on a pedestal. You climbed up, sat down and closed the sliding hatch. You were in a full-sized cockpit with all the standard instruments and controls. You could not see out.

It was a pneumatic and mechanical marvel, with very little electrical or electronics. The Link flew reasonably like an aircraft. It had motion in all three dimensions, so you could get vertigo. Many modern electronic simulators do not have motion, which is a mistake. The Links had the basic controls and instruments so we learned what it was like to control an aircraft in the clouds or at night, with no reference to the horizon.

Once we had completed a series of training sessions in the Link trainer, we practiced in the SNJ. In this phase, we sat in the backseat, with the instructor in the front seat. We were covered by a canvas enclosure that restricted all vision to the outside. This whole phase led up to the check ride, which tested us to the limit of our abilities.

This phase was not as long as the other phases, it was just 10 hops, so you had to progress rapidly. It began by practicing turns, glides, climbs and level flight all with a "full panel," that is, with the gyro instruments included. Then we would practice "partial panel," which used just the basic instruments, all the gyro instruments were turned off. Then we practiced what were called "Unusual Attitudes." "Unusual Attitudes" are any wing or nose position beyond 45 degrees. In training, we were usually placed on our back with the nose down in a dive or on our back with the nose up 45 degrees. These attitudes, unless corrected rapidly, lead to disaster.

I did very well in this phase, Lieutenant Anderle told me before my check ride, "Leue', you're my top student. I don't

Chapter 3   Basic Training, Pensacola   46

want you to just fly an 'Up,' I want to fly an 'Outstanding.'" I drew a Marine, CAPT Davis, for check pilot. The flight was in the afternoon in Pensacola. With many cumulus clouds in the area, the air was extremely rough.

My take off was flawless. The climb, the steep turns, the partial panel all went very well. CAPT Davis give me a partial panel unusual attitude on my back with my nose down. I quickly recovered, let down to the required altitude and turned to the compass heading required. The air was very rough, the wet compass was bouncing 10-15 degrees plus or minus, side to side. We returned and landed. Captain Davis said nothing during the entire flight.

Modern Weapons

We got out of the airplane and Lieutenant Anderle came out to greet us. Captain Davis said, "Midshipmen Leue,' I'm giving you a 'Down,' you were 15 degrees off heading in the Practical problem." I was stunned, and so was Lieutenant Anderle. Lieutenant Anderle walked back in with Captain Davis arguing with him all away, but he would not change his mind.

This meant I would have to fly two "Up" check rides, or be washed out of the program. Waiting to be scheduled for my first check ride, I couldn't sleep or eat. I was a wreck. I couldn't imagine washing out. I didn't know what I would do. I was so uptight, I could hardly walk, let alone fly.

I was scheduled for both check rides on the same day. Both flights were rough compared to the flight I had flown with CAPT Davis, but I was given an "Up" on both. Thank you Lord.

Getting a down was sobering, but I look back on it as a good experience. I was becoming overconfident and overconfidence, without great experience in aviation, is a deadly combination. In my Navy career, time and again, skill

Chapter 3   Basic Training, Pensacola

with instruments saved my life. The extra time and the kick in the pants, was good for me.

Radio

The remainder of the instrument syllabus was called "Radio." We were taught to fly instruments and to navigate by the use of the old Adcock radio range. These were low-frequency radio ranges that created four "beams" with an "A" (dit-da), in the East and West sectors and "N" (da-dit) in the North and South sectors

In the 1930s and 1940s, these ranges were the only means of radio navigation when on instruments. It required only a low-frequency receiver in the aircraft. The only input was audio, nothing visual. You found your position and kept track of it on a chart totally by what your ears told you.

We practiced finding our position by using a procedure called the "Fade 90 Orientation." First, we practiced in the Link trainer, then in the SNJ on the Pensacola range.

Flying in the SNJ, I first was required to go under my hood while still on the ground, Lt Anderle would then take off and fly to a position unknown to me, then say, "OK, Leue', you've got it, find your position, fly to the Pensacola range, make an approach to Pensacola Municipal Airport."

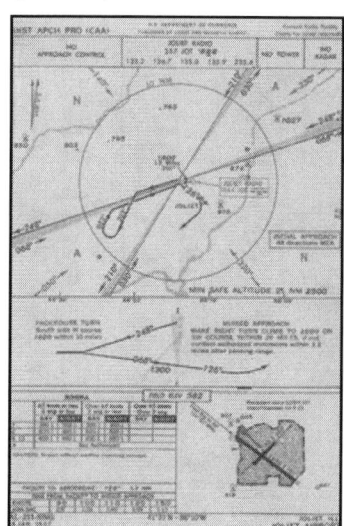

Adcock Range Plate

I was fascinated by this procedure. It was not difficult to learn. I easily passed "D" stage. I said "good-bye" to LT Anderle. He was an excellent instructor. I eagerly moved on to Saufley Field for training in Formation and Gunnery.

In the next ten years, the "Adcock Range," with its four quadrants and beams, totally disappeared from aviation. First,

CHAPTER 3   BASIC TRAINING, PENSACOLA   48

Adcock ranges were replaced with high frequency VOR "Omini" ranges, and ILS, Precision Instrument Landing Systems, followed by Global Positioning Systems, GPS.

Saufley Field—Formation

Up to this point in our training, we had been taught to stay well away from other aircraft. Now, we would be taught to fly very close together, in formation. Formation training started with flights of three aircraft, all duel, with an instructor in the backseat of each aircraft. We were briefed on the basics of controlling an aircraft on the wing of another aircraft. First, we had to learn how to join up, or rendezvous, with another aircraft. This was explained using a blackboard and chalk showing angles, the speeds and the techniques required.

On my first flight, the instructor demonstrated the rendezvous and proper wing position. He then turned over the controls to me and let me try flying wing. I recall when I was moving up on the other aircraft too fast, I instinctively put on the brakes. This is a common reaction from driving a car. Of course, the wheels and brakes were tucked away in the wing, and they were not about to slow down my aircraft. I had to pull back my throttle.

It took awhile to wire my left hand with the throttle to my brain until it moved instinctively to reduce power if I was over-running, and to add power if I was falling behind. I used my wings by banking subtly to move in or out to the correct distance.

Formation Training, Saufley Field

Flying wing is nothing more than coordinating the wings, to get closer or farther, the nose to go higher or lower, the

Chapter 3 Basic Training, Pensacola

throttle to go forward or backward. Soon this became instinctive, I didn't have to think about it.

Once we demonstrated the ability to hold a reasonable wing position, we would break up the flight and practice rendezvous. Learning to rendezvous took practice, trial and error. Rendezvous could be particularly dangerous because the rendezvousing aircraft approaches the lead aircraft from the side at a considerable closing speed. In a proper rendezvous the leader commences a left turn, the rendezvousing aircraft maneuvers to get on a 45-degree relative bearing on the inside of the circle, holding that bearing while closing the lead aircraft. As you close the lead aircraft, you have to match the lead aircraft's speed and wing position, crossing under him, then sliding to the outside wing position. We had several accidents during formation training, where students misjudged their speed and angle and flew into the lead aircraft.

Gunnery

Just like the other phases of instruction, Gunnery phase began with ground school, where we learned the basics of aerial gunnery on a blackboard. In this phase, we would be flying SNJs with a 30-caliber machine gun, firing through the propeller with a synchronizer. The SNJ had a fixed gun sight that projected on the wind-screen. The machine gun was fired by a trigger on the control stick. Safety was paramount. We were carefully briefed on when to arm and disarm the gun. We were taught about "Lead." "Lead" is the angle or distance you shoot in front of a moving target. The live Gunnery training was conducted in restricted areas out over the Gulf of Mexico.

Our instructor was Lt Daken. He was an excellent instructor and we all liked him very much. As a joke, we called him, "Down Check Daken." He was always positive, trying to teach us, anything but a "down check." In this picture, I am giving the "Down" check sign. I always felt bad about this—I hammed up a fine picture.

CHAPTER 3 BASIC TRAINING, PENSACOLA

Lt Daken Gunnery Flight

We were organized in flights of five. The instructor with a student in the backseat would take off first with a sleeved target under his wing. The other four students, with one designated as a leader, would take off and rendezvous on the instructor's wing. We climbed up to 5,000 feet heading out over the Gulf of Mexico. Lt Daken would signal the four shooters to climb 1000 feet and move out to what we called "The Perch," 1,000 feet up and about 500 yards to the right.

The instructor would stream the target sleeve on a cable several hundred yards in back of his aircraft. On signal, the shooters would peel off one at a time and dive on the target, firing when they were at 90 degrees deflection from the target. There was only a fleeting second to shoot, "rat, tat, tat, tat." Then you pulled out and climbed to a perch on the opposite side. We did this for six or eight runs, then joined up, put our guns on safe, then returned to Saufley Field.

Our hits were recorded according to the color that had been put on our bullets. Most of us took several flights to even record any hits. I loved this phase of training. I had been a hunter, I understood lead. I quickly rose to the top of my flight in hits.

We flew two to four flights a day. On every fourth flight, I flew in back of the tow plane with the instructor.

In our next phase, we would to go into carrier qualification training. We were bursting with fight and confidence.

Chapter 3   Basic Training, Pensacola

Night Flying

After completing our instrument training, we were scheduled for night flying during our formation and gunnery phases. This took place in the months of March through May 1949. The first two night flights with an instructor were called "safe for night solo checks." Instructors did not like these flights, they were the first flights a student flew at night. Everything is different at night. Usually there is no horizon and you have to rely on the flashlight in the cockpit to see things like switches and your maps. Also, the most prevalent accident in the SNJ was what we called a ground loop. A ground loop is losing control of the airplane on the runway when landing, winding up swerving left or right rapidly, scraping a wingtip. A tail wheel airplane like the SNJ naturally wants to go backwards, so you are constantly fighting to keep it straight on the runway. At night, it was easier for the airplane to get away. Also, landing the SNJ required that you slow down just above the runway in a three-point attitude, that is, touchdown with your tail wheel at the same time as the main mounts. If you leveled off too high, the SNJ would drop a wing as you fell through space, or at least it felt like it, before landing very hard, probably on one wheel or the other.

For these night flights, they would launch about 20 airplanes and put them in a circle a couple thousand feet over the field, then launch 20 more into a lower circle for landing. When the lower circle had completed several landings the upper circle would descend into the landing pattern and the lower circle would go up to the higher circle. Nobody liked night flying with this great mass of airplanes, flown primarily by students who had never been airborne at night before.

I completed my night safety checks on the night of March 8, 1949. Periodically, I would then be scheduled to fly solo at night practicing landings and simple navigation.

Jane and Mom Visit

During my Christmas leave, Jane and I planned that she and my mother would visit me in Pensacola sometime in the

Chapter 3 Basic Training, Pensacola 52

spring. Planning for that, I started to look for a car whenever I could get off the base for Liberty. I had been sending most of my paycheck home to Jane to keep in our joint account so I had very little available funds for a car.

I talked Gene Milway and another midshipman, now lost to my memory, into buying a car with me. The plan was we would share and share alike. We picked out a nice-looking used 1938 Plymouth business coup at a local used-car dealer. The car looked great, but it had some engine problems that I felt we could fix later on. I think we paid $400 for the car. As the time approached for Jane and my mother to arrive, Milway and my other friend agreed I could have the car exclusively during the period of time Jane and Mom were in Pensacola.

In early May, Jane, with mother as a chaperone, traveled by bus to Pensacola. Because I was now a Second-Class Midshipmen, I could go on Liberty during the week, if I had no flights. Since Jane and mother could only stay for a

Jane, Dave, Mom, Pensacola

- I put them up in at the Pensacola Motor Lodges, just off the main street in Pensacola on Palafox Avenue. Over the next week, we were able to explore the Pensacola beaches, Spanish Forts, restaurants and other attractions. Restaurants were an especially big treat, because in those days, we very seldom had the funds to eat out.

There was one particular restaurant in downtown Pensacola that served Southern fried chicken and Scuppernong wine.

Chapter 3 Basic Training, Pensacola

This was a big deal, because when did we ever have wine with dinner at home? Never.

We spent several days on the white sands and surf of Pensacola Beach. It was just a fabulous time and you can imagine how great it was to be with Jane after five months. Time just went too fast.

I was flying every day, so some days I didn't get to see Jane and Mom until in the evening.

Mon & Jane

On the night of May 5, 1949, I was scheduled for a night cross-country flight. Jane and Mother asked me whether they would see me that evening. I said, "I'll be out to see you," knowing that I had the night flight.

This particular flight was a short cross-country navigation flight, on a triangular track that went from Saufley Field to a small town in Alabama north of Pensacola, then to Mobile, Alabama, then back to Saufley Field. I briefed, manned up and was the very first aircraft to taxi out and take off. I stayed at maximum power and zipped around the course as fast as possible.

Mom & Dave

There was no radar in Pensacola in those days, and we were required to make position reports.

Dave & Jane

I reported in over Mobile, Alabama when I was over Pensacola, turned out my lights and dove down Palafox Avenue at treetop level.

The SNJ, when it was in low propeller pitch at full power made a terrific racket. After my flight, I landed and proceeded into town.

Jane, Pensacola

CHAPTER 3   BASIC TRAINING, PENSACOLA   54

Jane and Mom were sitting outside on the patio at the Pensacola Motor Lodges and Motel.

I asked them, "Did you see me?" They said, "Did we see you! We could see your face and all the numbers on your airplane!"

I realized what a dumb stunt this was. Anyone could have seen my number and reported me. I would've been sent home the next day. Also, I might easily have run into a tall tree or a telephone pole or an unlighted tower.

I never told any of my buddies, one of them would've spilled the beans. The only thing I can say is, I felt I had to do it.

I didn't know it at the time, but this was the beginning of my training for black-night attacks, which I would perfect seventeen years later burning enemy trucks on Vietnamese Highway One.

Carrier Qualification

Carrier Qualification, CQ, was the final phase of basic flight training. This phase began after gunnery and night flying and was the most intense phase of training. It began with ground school lectures explaining the traffic pattern, the speeds, altitudes and techniques of landing an aircraft on a ship. The carrier approach requires precise speed and altitude control while flying close to the ground in practice, or close to the water at sea.

The Landing Signal Officer, LSO, controlled each carrier approach and landing with signal paddles. However, you had to fly the aircraft and answer the LSO's signals precisely.

The basic signals were explained. "Roger," on speed and altitude, the LSO's paddles extended horizontally; "You are High," the LSO's arms raised 20° above the horizontal; "You are Low," the LSO's arms lowered 20° below the horizontal; "You are Fast," the LSO's right arm dropped 30°; "You are Slow," The LSO extends both arms toward the aircraft in a rowing motion; "Cut your engine, " the LSO's right arm

Chapter 3   Basic Training, Pensacola   55

crosses his neck; "Wave Off, go around," the LSO crosses both paddles over his head in a rapid fashion. The cut and the wave off are mandatory, but the other signals are recommendations.

Next, we were given a demonstration flight by an instructor who flew the carrier approach from the backseat and we observed from the front. We practiced on an airfield that had a simulated carrier deck painted on the runway.

My log book shows that this demo flight was given by a LT Lawrence on May 23, 1949. That same day I flew three more field carrier landing practice, FCLP, flights. On each of these flights, I made eight to ten practice carrier landings.

It was unnerving flying the SNJ so slow, and so close to the ground. Up until this phase all our flying had been well above the stall speed of the aircraft. Now we were flying at about 70 knots, 10 knots above the stall, at altitudes starting at 200 feet at the 180 degree point, down to 15 to 20 feet at the "Cut." It took concentration, guts and prayers to fly the aircraft at these altitudes and speeds through the turbulence of a Pensacola afternoon.

I flew four Field Carrier Landing Practice Flights (FCLP) flights a day for five days straight. In that period of time I made from 180 to 200 field carrier approaches and landings. Each pass or landing was graded by a critical Landing Signal Officer. Not until I could consistently fly a smooth, precise approach and landing would I be field qualified to go aboard the carrier. I was field qualified on May 27.

I boarded the carrier USS Wright at Pensacola, May 30, 1949. I felt confident and eager to try my hand at the ultimate in aviation skills, landing an aircraft on a ship. Of course, there were "butterflies." This would be a totally new experience. No matter how good the shore training, it could not duplicate a moving ship.

The USS Wright sortied the night of May 30, 1949. The ship was well out to sea in the Gulf of Mexico on the 31st of May.

CHAPTER 3 BASIC TRAINING, PENSACOLA 56

We arose early and had a hearty breakfast. We went to the ready room and were briefed by our LSOs. They briefed us on the deck launch procedures. We would be launched in groups of five or six, then stay in the pattern until we had made the six landings required for qualification.

I was in the first group to man up for launching. My heart was pounding as the signal was given to start engines. After warm up, I was given the pull chocks signal, then added power to follow the taxi signalman up the deck to the launching officer with the bold "Fly One" lettered on his yellow jersey.

I held the brakes, then quickly went over my checklist: fuel, flaps down, trim set, mixture rich, prop low pitch. I then looked at the Fly One who gave me the "Two finger" turn up signal. I advanced my throttle to 18 inches holding the brakes with the stick back, checked my magnetos, then nodded. The Fly One pointed down the deck. I "Two blocked" the throttle, full power, using right rudder as the tail came up angling toward the right side of the bow.

I was airborne well before the bow. I made a right clearing turn, then turned back to parallel the ship's course, climbing to 200 feet. At two ship lengths ahead of the bow, I commenced a left turn to the downwind checking wheels down, flaps down, hook down, mixture rich, prop low pitch.

SNJ Taking Off USS Wright, May 1949

CHAPTER 3 BASIC TRAINING, PENSACOLA 57

SNJ Approach USS Wright, May 1949

Downwind a-beam the island, I commenced my left turn towards the ship losing altitude to keep the ship's stack on the horizon. Passing through the 90 degree position, I picked up the LSO holding a "Roger."

Coming into "the groove," I received an easy "Come On" signal. I was slow, I corrected by adding a little power. The ship rushed toward me. The LSO gave me the "Cut." I closed the throttle, dropped my nose, then eased it back up, my hook grabbed a wire. Bam! I slammed into my shoulder straps. I was aboard!

A crewmen ran out in front of me with the "hook up" signal, then "hold your brakes" signal, then "taxi forward to the Fly

SNJ Landing USS Wright, May 1949

Chapter 3 Basic Training, Pensacola

One." Again I checked flaps down, fuel, mixture, prop, trim tabs, two finger turn up, then off again. I flew six straight approaches to "Cuts" and landings, without a wave-off. I was "Carrier qualified" within an hour. The Good Lord was steadying my hand.

After my last landing, they taxied me forward, they chocked up the airplane with the engine running, I unstrapped, climbed out, then another pilot jumped in for his six landings.

The LSO debriefed me later in the ready room. I had flown six OK passes. I was elated beyond description, I had overcome my fears, excelled, and even had fun.

This was a mighty big step in my life.

On to advanced training.

CHAPTER FOUR

Advanced Training

Pensacola to Corpus Christi, Texas

What would I fly?

A Fighter Pilot?

At this point, I was not sure what type of aircraft I would fly in advanced training. The type of aircraft selected was very important for career considerations. It would determine what kind of ship I would serve in, what my duties would be, as well as influence my entire Navy career.

Middies at Pensacola Beach

For many months, my fellow Midshipmen and I had heated discussions as to the best career path. We had the choice of several types of aircraft: fighters, sea planes, or multi-engine patrol planes.

My plan since high school was to be an airline pilot. In discussions with my roommate, Gene Milway, I argued that the best choice would be to put in for multi-engine training. Despite my arguments, both of us knew fighters would be much more fun to fly. The SNJ we were flying was like a little fighter. We both loved it. Fighters fit our personalities.

Still, I argued, "Who will want a fighter pilot when we get out of the Navy?" I said, "Milway, let's put in for multi-engines, then we'll be in good shape to fly for the airlines if and when we decide to get out." Finally, he agreed and we both put in our requests for multi-engine training. Almost everybody

CHAPTER 4   ADVANCED TRAINING

wanted fighters, so we were sure we would get our requests for multi-engines. These assignments were always made immediately after completing basic carrier qualification.

About this time I bought out my partners in 1938 Plymouth, it was now mine and I decided to overhaul it during carrier qualifications. Late one afternoon, shortly after completing my carrier qualifications, I was at the base hobby shop, under my car, working furiously to get the engine back together. Jim Carr walked up, looked under the car and announced, "I was over at the office and I found out your assignment!" I was certain I would get either P2V or PB4Y-2 patrol planes. I said, "Well Jim, what did I get?" He said, "You got Corsairs!" I said, "Damn it!" I threw the wrench in my hand with all my might. The wrench clanged repeatedly, ricocheting off of the chassis several times, coming back and almost hitting me.

I lay there for a moment under the car, in the semi-darkness and said to myself, "OK, Lord, I'll be a fighter pilot." I never looked back, I was never sorry. Fighters fit my personality. I would never have been happy in patrol planes. This meant I'd be going to Cabiness Field, near Corpus Christi, Texas. Now I had to finish putting my car together!

Milway got PB4Y-2 patrol planes and went on to the airlines.

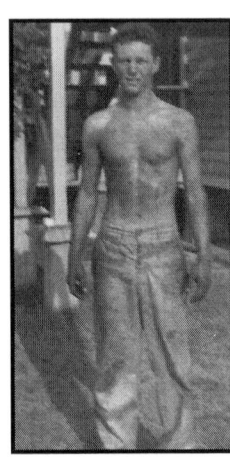

Part-time Mechanic

I found out later that the Navy was concerned with the high accident rate of Corsair pilots in training. They picked Midshipmen with the best flight scores and put them in Corsairs.

I finished my Plymouth engine at the last minute, but I could not get it started. I quickly wore my battery down trying. I asked another Midshipman friend, Don Llewellyn, for a push with his car. He pushed me and pushed me, to no avail. It still would not start. Finally, late at night, I gave up.

Chapter 4   Advanced Training

The next morning, I checked everything and found that a wire in the distributor was shorting out. I finally got it started. It ran, but it didn't sound good. I had to take it as it was. I was out of time. I cleaned up the car, packed my gear, and got underway as the sun was setting. I believe the date was June 3, 1949. I had three days to get to Corpus Christi.

All my other buddies had opted for more reliable transportation. My roommate, Johnny Thompson, would be driving his new 1949 Dodge sedan. I had been sending all my money home to Jane to put in her hope chest, so I was in no financial condition to drive anything better than my 1938 Plymouth.

I departed on a pitch black night. About an hour into the trip, the engine made a loud bang and backfire, the car slowed and would not go over 20 to 25 miles an hour. I stopped and looked under the hood, but could find nothing obvious, so I set off again. It would bang and backfire terribly as I'd try to accelerate. I could not go over 25 miles an hour. I imagined that an intake valve had stuck open and it was backfiring through the carburetor.

I pulled into a little gas station in the middle of nowhere. I told the local mechanic the symptoms and asked his advice. He said, "It's your timing chain." I said, "I think its a stuck intake valve." He said, "No, it's your timing chain." I asked how much it would cost to have it fixed. I have forgotten the stated amount, but it far exceeded the cash I had with me, which was just enough for gas and food along the way. I didn't have even have enough money to stop at a hotel. While this conversation was going on, I noticed a soldier standing nearby listening.

When the mechanic and I were finished, I said, "Well I'll just have to drive it as it is." The soldier asked me where I was going. I told him, "Corpus Christi, Texas." He said, "That's where I'm going, can I have a ride? I'll help you with the gas." I thought for a minute. It was night, in the middle of nowhere. I certainly never saw this soldier before, I was uneasy taking him. But, maybe I would need some help with

CHAPTER 4   ADVANCED TRAINING

the gas money. I said, "I've got real problems with his car, but you are welcome to come along."

We got underway banging and backfiring. I had no tools, not even a plug wrench, to check out my theory of the stuck intake valve. The mechanic convinced me that I was wrong. We drove on in to the night, through Mobile, Alabama, New Orleans and on. When I stopped for gas, I noticed that the engine was dripping quantities of oil in addition to its other problems. I had to put in a couple quarts of oil at each stop. In the early morning I stopped for gas on the other side of New Orleans, the soldier thanked me and said he would look for a faster ride. I plugged along until I was in the outskirts of Houston, Texas. At each gas stop, I was putting in more oil. I was using so much oil, I was running out of money. I had to do something about the oil or I would not make Cabaniss Field. Finally, in the morning, west of Houston, I stopped at a little one-pump gas station, in the middle of nowhere, Texas.

A New Friend

There was a young Negro man working alone at the gas station. I told him the problems I was having with my engine. He put my car up on an outside lift in the back of the station. He looked under the engine and said, "You need a new rear oil seal." I said, "How much will it cost and how fast can you do the job? I am almost out of money and I need to be in Corpus Christi by tomorrow night." He quoted a very reasonable price and said he could order the seal and have it delivered by Greyhound bus from Houston, by two o'clock that afternoon. I said, "OK, do it!"

He was a very personable, friendly young man. We talked and kidded as I waited. At times I helped him service cars that stopped. Finally, he said, "Would you watch the station for awhile? I have to go see my girlfriend." I was surprised, but said, "Sure." He went off for an hour or two, while I ran the gas station!

A little after noon, my new friend came back. At two o'clock, the Greyhound bus stopped with my part. He dropped the oil pan then quickly installed the new oil seal. Toward evening, I was ready to go again. I paid my bill and thanked my friend. I felt good. I cleaned up in the restroom and put on my good pants and shoes. I was going to do the last lap to Corpus Christi in style.

A Night to Remember

About an hour later, the sun was setting and I tried to turn on my lights. The lights didn't go on. I pulled off on the right side of the dark road, fifty or so miles west of Houston. There were no houses or any civilization from horizon to horizon. There was a railroad track about a quarter-mile to the right (north). It had been raining and the shoulder on the side of the road was slick Texas red clay. I fiddled with the wiring harness under the hood and got the lights working. I got back in, started up and tried to drive back up on the road, but the slick Texas red clay was just like grease. The car slowly slid farther and farther down the slope until I was twenty five to thirty feet from the road, stuck in the mud. It was now dark as pitch with no moon.

There was absolutely no traffic. I looked off to the right toward the railroad tracks and there was an abandoned oil well. I walked down the hill and saw that there were planks of wood laying around. I made several trips pulling these planks up to the car and laid them out like a driveway back up to the road. This took me an hour or two. I was muddy and tired when I finished. I started the car and tried to drive it up the driveway by placing rocks and gravel under the back wheels for traction. The car just didn't have enough power to drive up my makeshift driveway.

Dave's 1938 Plymouth

My good shoes were muddy and my good pants were a mess. I was dead tired and discouraged. I fell asleep in the front seat. The only traffic was an occasional huge truck, pulling an oil well rig. These rigs would appear first as a faint light flickering on the horizon, gradually getting brighter, louder and louder, then thundering by, then slowly fading to the other horizon. It was eerie. I awoke at about 2 a.m. I decided if another oil well truck came by, I would stand out in the road and flag it down. Soon a flickering light appeared in the east. As the rig approached I stood out in the road, waving my arms. I did this with some trepidation and quickly stepped to the side of the road. A large rig braked to a screeching halt as it went by me. I walked to the cab. The window rolled down, and a gruff, but friendly, voice asked, "What's your problem, buddy? Can I help you?" I said, "My car's stuck down there," pointing into the darkness. He got a big rope, tied it from his rig to my bumper and pulled me out of there in nothing flat. I thanked him profusely. He roared off into the night and I proceeded on my way at 25 mph, being sure not to get off the road again.

Johnny Thompson

Early the next morning, about 6 a.m., I was poking along at 25 miles an hour when I heard, "Beep, beep." I looked in the rearview mirror. To my great surprise and joy, it was my roommate and good friend, Johnny Thompson. He had departed Pensacola a day after me. He could see I was in trouble, poking along with smoke trailing behind me. I drove to a safe spot, pulled over and told him my problems. We decided to go to the next town and have breakfast and talk it over. We pulled into a little Texas diner, and had a great

Naval Auxiliary Air Station Cabaniss Field, Texas

CHAPTER 4   ADVANCED TRAINING

breakfast. Johnny loaned me $20 for gas and oil. He decided that he'd continue on his way and if I didn't show up by that evening, he'd come back and rescue me. I felt great. I plugged away and finally made it to Corpus Christi that afternoon. I stopped briefly, then travelled the last 30 miles to Naval Auxiliary Air Station Cabaniss Field, Texas. I checked in with the Officer of the Day, found the barracks I'd be staying in, carried my gear in and parked my Plymouth. I never wanted to see it again.

I would be rooming with Johnny Thompson, "Rube" Brogan, John Kordeleski, Bernie Shank and Tom Cawley. I was happy I was among my friends, and we were now all First-Class Midshipman, almost officers. Soon we would be flying the vaunted Corsair.

The Corsair

Upon checking in at Cabaniss Field, we were informed that the Navy Brass, in another attempt to reduce the accident rate in Corsairs, planned to have our class fly the F6F Hellcat, a more docile fighter, before we flew the Corsair. We spent a week in ground school, learning all of the systems in the F6F: the engine, the hydraulic system, the fuel system, the controls and flight characteristics. We were tested on our knowledge, then the next day we were told to report to the hangar for our first familiarized flight. We all showed up bright and early, eager to start flying. We were told to stand by, there would be a delay. We waited on the flight line for more than an hour. We were then called back to the ready room, where our instructors told us the "powers-that-be" had changed their minds. We would not fly the Hellcat, we would start Corsair ground school immediately.

F4U-4 Corsair

CHAPTER 4   ADVANCED TRAINING   66

Out of Gas

The next "bombshell" was announced shortly thereafter. We were told the Navy was out of money until July 1st, the beginning of the fiscal year. We were all given 10 days leave! We could go home or do whatever we wanted, but there was no money to buy gas or to pay us. Louis Johnson, the Secretary of Defense, under President Harry Truman, had cut the military budget to bare bones and we were feeling the pinch.

Of course, all of us wanted to travel to see our families and our sweethearts. I had only seen Jane twice since starting flight training in May 1948. My roommate, Tom Cawley said, "Hey, Leue' you've got a car. Let's drive it to Buffalo, New York. I can hitchhike to New Jersey from there." I explained the condition of my car to Tom and said, "There is no way that car can make it to New York, besides it only goes 25 miles an hour." Nevertheless, I told him we could work on it that night and see what happens. We stayed up late working under the car. We dropped the pan on the engine, shimmed up the bearings and resealed the pan. I checked the valves, and sure enough, I was right, there was a stuck intake valve. We fixed the valve, then started it. Amazingly, it didn't run too bad.

We agreed we would make a decision in the morning. Cawley and I went to bed after midnight. In the cold light of morning, we tested the car by driving it toward the main base, Naval Air Station Corpus Christi. It ran a lot better than on my trip from Pensacola, however, we agreed it would probably never make it to Buffalo. The rod bearings clattered and it sounded awful, although it would go 50 or 60 miles an hour. Since we were at Naval Air Station Corpus Christi, we decided to check on flights. Tom Cawley was a smooth talker. He quickly made friends with the pilot of a PB4Y-2 that was going to Pawtuxet River, Maryland. The pilot said he had room for us. We asked him what his takeoff time was, he said in one hour. That meant we would have to

Chapter 4   Advanced Training   67

return the 30 miles to Cabaniss Field, pack our gear and come back, all in one hour's time.

The math didn't compute, but we ran out the door and jumped in my 1938 Plymouth. I wound it up as tight as it would go. I was surprised, I had it going about 70 on the straight road to Cabaniss Field. For a while we were doing OK. However, that old engine did not have a pressure lubrication system, it had what was called "splash lubrication." We had just shimmed up the rod bearings the night before. Soon, we could hear the rod bearings start to burn and clatter louder and louder, still I kept the accelerator on the floor.

Smoke was coming up through the floor boards, the rods were making a terrible din. The hangars of Cabaniss were looming up ahead. Cawley and I were cheering on the old 1938 Plymouth. Almost every cent I had in the world was in that car, but I didn't care, I was going home to see Jane. The smoke got so thick that we rolled the windows down to put our heads out the window. Suddenly, there was a tremendous bang and clatter. The engine quit. I put the clutch in, and we coasted for about a mile. I looked back and I saw parts dancing in the road with a swath of oil stretching a quarter-mile in back of us. The engine had thrown a rod right out through the side of the block. I pulled off to the side of the road and came to a stop. We jumped out, locked the car and put out our thumbs.

The next car heading for Cabaniss picked us up. I ran to the barracks and packed our gear. Cawley ran to Administration and got our leave papers. A friend, Don Llewellyn, was there. I offered him $10 if he would drive us to Corpus Christi, fast. He had a fast car. We piled in and roared past my 1938 Plymouth with the swath of oil and parts down the road. Don Llewellyn made record time, but just as we pulled up to the Marines at the Corpus Christi Naval Air Station gate, a PB4Y-2 thundered over our heads.

We had missed our flight.

Chapter 4   Advanced Training

I paid and thanked Don Llewellyn after he dropped us off at Station operations. We inquired if there were any other flights scheduled later that day. There was only a Navy R4D (DC-3) going to San Antonio Air Force Base in an hour. We signed up for the flight. We didn't know exactly where we were going, but we were going. When we got to San Antonio we were startled to find that most of our Flying Midshipmen buddies from Cabaniss had driven to San Antonio the night before, and were already on the list for flights. Cawley and I were placed on the bottom of the list. At 5 p.m. in the evening they closed the Operations office.

We were told to come back in the morning at 8 o'clock. They warned us that anyone found hanging around the flight line would be escorted off the base.

Cawley and I decided our only chance to get home would be to go down to the flight line anyway, and try to catch a flight that night to anywhere back East. It was a pleasant evening. We rested on benches, talked about our girlfriends and waited for incoming flights. About midnight, a B-29 bomber landed. We went to the chow hall to have Mid-rats (chow) with the crew. Cawley found out that the pilot was from his hometown in New Jersey. He made friends with the pilot, who said he was leaving at 7 in the morning. The pilot promised to get us on board, not to worry about the Operations people.

True to his word, the pilot and crew showed up at seven. He got us on board the B-29. Later, the Ops people loaded more of our buddies, who had been waiting in Operations the day before. We roared off heading for Detroit, Michigan. All went well until we came to a cold front with embedded thunderstorms. The turbulence was terrible. The pilot ordered everyone to put on parachutes. This was a lark for us. Here we were about to jump out of an Air Force bomber. We were hit by lightning and violently bounced about, but the pilot did a good job and flew out of the front, landing safely in Detroit. The B-29 had holes in the wing from the lightning. From Detroit, both Cawley and I took trains, I to Buffalo and he to New Jersey.

CHAPTER 4 ADVANCED TRAINING

I called Jane from Detroit and arrived in Buffalo the next morning. Jane and I were both excited. This was an unexpected treat. We had a great week together visiting family and friends, enjoying just being together. We took a day trip to Niagara Falls, where I took this picture. It is one of my favorite pictures of her. After a week or so, Arnold Febrey, my future father-in-law, became concerned that I wasn't going to make it back to Corpus Christi, Texas on time. He knew that I had no money to fly or take a train. I said, "No problem. I'll catch a flight out of the Naval Air Station, Niagara Falls." Really, he was absolutely right, but with the optimism of youth, I wasn't worried at all.

Jane, Niagara Falls,

Finally, two days before I had to be back, Arnold and Jane drove me to the Niagara Falls Naval Air Station. I immediately went to the Operations office and told them that I was looking for a flight going anywhere West, I was trying to get to Corpus Christi, Texas. The Petty Officer at the desk said ,"There is a twin Beechcraft taxiing out for takeoff right now, going to Olathe, Kansas." He called the tower to see if they would hold the Beechcraft. The tower called the pilot and he held at the end of the runway. I said hasty goodbyes to Jane and family. I was driven out to the airplane in a jeep and I climbed in. The pilots were two fighter pilots getting their flight time. After we were airborne, we chatted for a time. I told them that I was in flight training and going to fly Corsairs. They told me of their experiences. I fell asleep, having gotten very little rest during my brief visit with Jane.

I woke up when we landed in Chicago, not a very good landing. The twin Beechcraft was not an easy aircraft to land. After refueling, we headed for Olathe, Kansas. I again fell asleep. The next thing I knew, we were at the Naval Air

CHAPTER 4   ADVANCED TRAINING

Station Olathe, Kansas. I thanked the pilots profusely and checked in at the Operations desk to see if there are any flights to Corpus Christi, Texas.

There was also another Flying Midshipman waiting for a flight to Corpus Christi. The Second Class Petty Officer at the Ops desk was a friendly fellow and he would ask all reserve pilots planning a flight if they would take us to Corpus Christi, Texas. Several came and went during the afternoon, but none wanted to fly to Corpus Christi, Texas. Finally, the Operations Petty Officer talked a pilot of a SNJ into flying as far south as Dallas, Texas. That's as far as he would go, and he could only take one of us. Since my fellow Flying Midshipman was there first, he got the ride to Dallas.

I was feeling quite sorry for myself as the afternoon droned on with no prospects going south to Corpus Christi. Finally, I had almost given up hope, when a Reserve Lieutenant came in to fly a TBM torpedo bomber. The Operations Petty Officer told him my plight and the Lieutenant said, "Sure, I'll take him right to Cabaniss field if he wants. I need the flight time." As we were walking out to the aircraft I told the Lieutenant about my buddy in Dallas. The Lieutenant said, "I'll stop there for fuel and will pick him up." I climbed into the TBM turret facing backwards, something I always wanted to do.

It was a beautiful afternoon. We took off heading south towards Dallas in high spirits. The TBM cruised about 200 miles an hour, so we were in Dallas in no time. We landed and I told the pilot I'd like to play a joke on my buddy. I'd tell him that we had no room in the plane, and then as we are walking out to the aircraft, I'll go back and tell him there was room for him. I went into the Operations office and there was my Flying Midshipman buddy sitting dejectedly. I told him I had a ride in the TBM directly to Cabaniss, but it was too bad, there was only space for me. After the pilot had fueled the aircraft, I started to walk out toward the TBM, then I went back for my buddy and said, "Come on, I was only kidding. We're going directly to Cabaniss." Everyone had a good laugh. We were both going to make it back on time. The flight to Cabaniss was only an hour and a half. We thanked our

Chapter 4 — Advanced Training

Reserve Lieutenant for his efforts and checked in with the duty officer with several hours to spare.

Preparing to fly the F4U-4 Corsair

I approached flying the Corsair with great enthusiasm and great respect. I had read much as a teenager about this great fighter. It had an awesome reputation for performance, but I also knew that it had a reputation as a killer. It wasn't called "The Bent Wing Ensign Eliminator," "Hose Nose" or "Widow Maker" for nothing. Still fresh in my mind was an incident that took place when I was in Preflight. I had shared a taxi going into town with two Second Class Midshipmen, who were waiting for their aircraft assignments. The Commanding Officer of a reserve Corsair squadron had just been killed landing a Corsair on a carrier off of Pensacola. This accident was common knowledge and these Midshipmen were discussing the possibilities of being assigned Corsairs. One said, "If an experienced Commanding Officer kills himself in that monster, what chance has a Midshipman got? I don't care what they do to me. I won't fly that airplane, I'll quit the program!"

We began ground school learning all the details of the Corsair's construction and flight characteristics. I paid rapt attention. In two weeks of ground school, we learned every detail of the systems of the aircraft. We learned the operation of the engine, the fuel system, the hydraulic system, the electrical system and the gun system. The hydraulic system was engine driven, with an electrical pump and hand pump for backup. The hydraulic system operated the landing gear flaps, wing flaps, tail-hook and intercooler doors.

We learned the Corsair was a single-seat shipboard fighter with folding wings, powered by a R-2800-18 W Pratt Whitney piston engine of 2,250-horsepower. It had a two-stage, two-speed supercharger that could maintain takeoff power up to 28,000 feet. Takeoff power settings were manifold pressure, 54 inches of mercury, with 2,800 rpm. War Emergency power, limited to five minutes, was 70 inches of manifold pressure, with water injection. It had a four-bladed Hamilton Standard propeller of 14 feet diameter. Its top speed at 28,000 feet altitude was more than 420 miles an hour. The Corsair carried six 50-caliber machine guns, three in each wing outboard of the propeller arc. The guns were bore-sited to converge 800 feet in front of the aircraft. It carried 400 rounds of 50-caliber ammunition for each gun, 2,400 rounds total. Rate of fire of each gun was 600 rounds a minute. The Corsair had two fuselage bomb racks and eight wing rocket/bomb racks. The Corsair carried 235 gallons of 115 /145 octane aviation fuel in a single self-sealing fuel tank immediately in front of the pilot. It had armor plate in back of the pilot and under the pilot.

We learned in detail the flight characteristics and the limitations of the aircraft. The Corsair was stressed for over nine positive and three negative Gees. It was a very strong aircraft. Our ground instructors were top Navy Petty Officers, who had spent years working on Corsairs. The flight characteristics were taught by top Navy fighter pilots. The major caution was to avoid spins. Spins in a Corsair were hard, if not impossible to recover from, and almost always fatal. The pre-curser to a spin is always a stall, so stalls and stall warnings were reviewed at length.

At the end of our two-week ground school we were given a blindfold cockpit check, then we were allowed to start and taxi the Corsair. The Corsair had a long nose extending more than 10 feet in front of the pilot blocking foreword vision on the ground. We learned to taxi by constantly "S" turning, weaving back and forth, always looking out the left or right side. We were cautioned not to ride the brakes because they would easily overheat.

Each flight instructor was given seven Midshipmen to train. Including the instructor, each flight made two divisions of four. In the Navy, a four-plane division is the standard tactical element. Our instructor's name was Lt. Forkner. He was an outstanding fighter pilot and instructor. Prior to our initial flight in the Corsair, LT Forkner gave us a long, detailed briefing. Each one of us knew that this flight would be one of

CHAPTER 4   ADVANCED TRAINING

the most challenging flights in our careers. We all had about two hundred flight hours flight time in the 650-horsepower SNJ. Now we were about to embark on a flight in a 2,250-horse power fighter alone! There were no simulators or two seat Corsairs.

It was get in, fly it, or die. On our initial flight, LT Forkner briefed that we were to start up then taxi behind him to the end of the takeoff runway. He would pull off to the side of the runway and watch each of our takeoffs, then he would takeoff and follow us. We would join up in a loose tail chase, fly to an outlying field and circle. LT Forkner would land first then each of us would make approaches for touch-and-go landings as he observed. After landing practice we were to go individually to a clear area to practice maneuvers in the aircraft, then return individually to Cabaniss field for a final landing.

The day before my first flight, my roommates, Tom Cawley and Jim Brogan, made their first flights in the Corsair. Cawley was bragging before his flight and said, "Watch my takeoff. I'm going to suck the gear right out from underneath me." I rounded up a group of Middies and we went out

Johnny Thompson, Tom Cawley, Dave Leue & Jim Brogan

CHAPTER 4   ADVANCED TRAINING   74

beside the runway to watch Cawley. Cawley added power and roared down the runway. We all watched him intently. He got airborne in a wobbly fashion, and went out of sight, with his gear down! We all rolled on the ground, laughing. However, what happened next in Cawley's flight, was not a laughing matter. Two of the pilots in his flight had a midair collision, one pilot bailed out, the other made a crash landing on the beach on Padre Island. At that time, Padre Island was uninhabited. Fortunately, neither pilot was injured

First Corsair Flight

On August 1, 1949, our flight followed LT Forkner's briefing exactly. The events of Cawley and Brogan's flight were fresh in my mind. However, I resolved to fly the Corsair, come what may. I started the big R-2800 Pratt Whitney with no problems and taxied out in order. When my turn for takeoff came, my heart was pounding. I pulled onto the runway, locked my tail wheel, locked open the canopy, glanced through the check-off list and smoothly added power feeding in right rudder to control the torque of the big prop.

As the tail came up, roaring down the runway, the Corsair felt solid and firm compared to the SNJ, a little back stick, and away it went. I picked up the gear. It accelerated rapidly, and felt very stable and precise to control. I pulled up in a loose tail chase in back of the plane ahead of me and switched to the assigned frequency. Lt. Forkner had us check in one by one. He flew up alongside directing us to the outlying field. He pulled ahead, circled, then landed. We flew overhead in a tail chase, broke into the downwind one by one. When my turn came, I made a left break behind the aircraft ahead of me, power to 18 inches, gear down, cranked open the canopy, then flaps down, mixture rich, prop low pitch, cowl flaps open, check list complete. Easy left turn, airspeed 90 knots, held 90 knots until crossing the threshold, nose coming up, power coming back, touchdown, roll a little, full power, re-trim, go around and do it again.

After three touch and goes we were allowed to fly out into a practice area and feel the airplane out. I did mild aerobatic

Chapter 4   Advanced Training   75

F4U-4, Midshipman Dave Leue', 1949

maneuvers, then tested the slow flight characteristics, opening the throttle to see what it would do. The Corsair had a very high rate of roll for a prop fighter. It also had a great high-speed stall warning. Approaching the stall, the whole airplane would shake. A very positive stall warning. Very comforting. I lost some of my fear. I practiced some slow flight, but we were cautioned never to stall the Corsair with gear and flaps down. I returned to Cabaniss, entered the pattern, broke and landed, taxied in. I had flown the storied Corsair. I loved it.

At this point, the pace of training picked up. We flew an average of one to two training flights each day. Each flight was preceded by at least an hour's briefing covering the flight in detail. After the flight, there was a half hour of debriefing. So, getting into flight gear, briefing, flying, debriefing and getting out of flight gear took four or five hours.

The weather in Texas in August was very, very hot and humid, and the Corsair was not air-conditioned. We would return after each flight with flight suits soaking with perspiration.

The next several flights were familiarization flights, flying formation with a wingman, learning more about the Corsair's flight characteristics, learning about the local training area. I recall flying wing on Bernie Shank when suddenly I got tears in my eyes. The realization that I was flying the legendary Corsair, instead of dreaming about it, just swept over me. I was quickly building confidence in myself and the airplane.

Chapter 4   Advanced Training   76

The Skyrocket

About this time, I discovered a skyrocket in my dresser drawer. I had purchased it for the Fourth of July, but hadn't used it because of our leave when the Navy ran out of gas. There was a strict rule on the base: No Fireworks. We set them off occasionally, just to harass the Marines.

I showed my skyrocket to Tom Cawley. We both thought it would be good fun to stir up the Marines. After it was dark, Cawley and I went up on our barracks' outside stairs to the second-story landing. The wind was blowing quite hard, which made it difficult to set up the skyrocket against the railing. We wanted to aim the rocket so it would arc out over the base. I finally got it in a good position and lit the fuse. Cawley and I ran to the other end of the barracks to watch. We heard it go off, but didn't see the rocket go up into the night sky. We didn't want to return to the scene of the crime immediately, so we went to our room. In a minute or two, our curiosity got the best of us. We went upstairs to look for the skyrocket. At first we saw nothing, then we noticed a hole in an open window screen, the skyrocket tail was sticking out, we rushed into the room. The wind had blown over the skyrocket and it had fired its load of pyrotechnics right into a room instead of the sky! The mattress on the upper bunk was on fire. There was a Midshipman snoozing in the lower bunk. We escorted him out of the room, grabbed the burning mattress, and beat out the fire. Fortunately, the Marines did not discover our shenanigans, nor did we burn down the barracks. Neither would have been good.

Dive Bombing and Gunnery

After the familiarization stage, we went immediately into dive bombing. The Corsair was an excellent pure fighter during World War II, but the reason that it remained valuable to the Navy for many years was because it also was an excellent dive bomber. The Navy taught dive bombing exclusively. If you dove the aircraft at the target at the proper angle, the proper speed and released at the proper altitude, your bomb would hit the target.

Chapter 4   Advanced Training

The first bombing run we learned was diving at a 45 degree angle, clean, with landing gear up, from an altitude of 8,000 feet. We commenced the dive bombing run by flying the aircraft to a point on a 45° cone around the target at 8,000 feet. At that point, we rolled on our back, pulled the nose down to the target then rolled the wings level, diving at the target while maintaining the dive angle, keeping the sight on the target and closely monitoring altitude. Pull out began at 2,500 feet. It required the immediate application of back stick to get and hold five to seven Gees. Minimum pullout altitude was 1,000 feet. Any pullout below 1,000 feet was a "low pullout," the instructor was orbiting at that altitude. A low pullout would get a below-average grade on your flight write up. Consistent low pullouts would get you a disposition board and maybe a trip home. A really low pullout would get you a trip home in a box.

It sounded easy, but we found dive bombing required intensive training to gain the skills necessary to hit accurately on a consistent basis. It required courage, skill and precision to recognize the proper dive angle, the correct

LT Forkner's Corsair flight, Cabaniss Field, Texas, September 1949

Top: LTJG Fritzie, Mid'n Goodman, Mid'n Rudy Krause, ENS Kramer

Bottom: Mid'n Dave Leue', Mid'n Emmet Alaud, Mid'n Bernie Shank

CHAPTER 4   ADVANCED TRAINING   78

airspeed and altitude to "pickle," or drop, descending at 20,000 feet per minute at speeds of more than 400 miles an hour.

On our bombing flights, each aircraft carried six or eight small Mark 76 practice bombs with smoke grenades. Before take off, we pre-computed our sight settings for the dive angle, the release altitude and the type of bomb. Our gun and bomb site was called a "reflecting sight," it projected red bull's eye rings on our wind screen. The rings were spaced in "mils," or thousandths of a circle. A typical site setting for 45 degree bombing was 100 mils. We would take off in a flight of eight, join up and proceed to the bombing range, which was a large bull's eye inscribed on the desert. It had white chalk rings at 25, 50, 100 and 200 feet. We would commence our dive bombing by flying across the target then breaking up into a left-hand pattern with an interval close enough to keep the aircraft in front of you in sight. This was very important. If you lost sight of the aircraft in front of you, you could easily turn too soon, then fly into your buddy ahead. As they say, "A mid-air collision will ruin your whole day." Each aircraft would call, "Number so and so, rolling in." After each run we would call, "Number so and so, is off." In that way we could keep track of others in the flight.

The range was manned by sailors who would call off the hit or the miss distance after each dive-bombing run. We completed several flights doing 45 degree dive bombing then we graduated to 60 degree dive bombing. In the 60 degree dive bombing, we put down our landing gear to act as speed brakes. This was important because in a 60 degree dive from 10,000 feet commencing pullout at 2,500 feet, without the landing gear, you would be going so fast you probably could not pull out. The Corsair's landing gear was unique in that it could be put down at any speed. You could not hurt the landing gear. Every other airplane I've ever flown had a speed restriction on lowering the landing gear. The Corsair's landing gear was designed as a speed brake. This was unique among propeller fighters. It also made the Corsair a superior dive bomber.

CHAPTER 4 ADVANCED TRAINING

We flew dive bombing missions day after day interspersed with tactics, night flying and navigation flights throughout the months of August and September. The weather was perfect and the days just flew by. The syllabus at Cabaniss required about 100 hours of flight training.

The final flights were tactics and gunnery. We were taught the "Thatch Weave," a fighter tactic, developed by Lieutenant, later Admiral, Thatch, to combat the Japanese Zero fighter. There were series of aerial gunnery flights, where we fired at banners towed by another Corsair out over the Gulf of Mexico.

On one of these flights, I experienced my first case of blacking out. I pulled too many Gees too long coming out of a gunnery run. I woke up, I imagine in seconds, but I was not sure where I was or what I was doing. Fortunately, we were at 10,000 feet. I found the flight, then continued the gunnery runs, being more careful pulling Gees. Later, in the fleet we would be issued "Gee Suits" that would increase our Gee tolerance. Following aerial gunnery we completed our gunnery training in ground strafing with the Corsair's 50 caliber machine guns.

Goodbye Plymouth

I had left my 1938 Plymouth on the side of the road going to Corpus Christi when Tom Cawley and I blew up the engine on our Gas Leave. Occasionally, during August and September, one of my buddies would needle me, "Where is your car, Leue'?" I'd say, "I don't know and I don't care." One Sunday going into town with Ned Steiner, we went looking for my old 1938 Plymouth. All that was left was a swath of oil on the road where it had died. Steiner took me into town, where I inquired at the local police station. They directed me to their impound yard. My 1938 Plymouth sat forlornly in the impound yard with a note under the windshield wiper. It read, "I have a new Plymouth engine. If you want to sell this car, call me." There was a phone number. I called the number and introduced myself as the owner the 1938 Plymouth. We negotiated and the gentleman bought my Plymouth for $250. I was happy and he was happy. It was a beautiful little car and now it had a new owner and a new engine.

Dixieland

On most weekends, I stayed on base. Frequently, I would listen to powerful nighttime AM stations out of Dallas or New Orleans, which played "Dixieland." I recall hearing the Dixie tune, "When the War breaks out in Mexico, I'm going to Montréal." Ironically, this comical theme became reality years later during the Vietnam war. I also heard, "Big Noise from Winnetka," a great Dixieland instrumental by Bob Crosby. After hearing that for the first time I sat down and wrote my dear Aunt Lorett in Winnetka, Illinois, which I'm sure was a great shock to her. She, my Uncle Alf and Cousin Carol, had kept me and loved me for more than two years after my father died. She had always treated me as a son. I seldom wrote or communicated my thankfulness to her.

Gene Milway

One of our final training flights in the Corsair was a cross country to Dallas, Texas. We stayed overnight in Dallas, then flew back the next day. I met my old Basic Training roommate, Gene Milway, who had also flown to Dallas as a member of the crew of a PB4Y-2 patrol bomber. We went on liberty together that night in Dallas. The next day, as we were departing, I noticed Milway's PB4Y-2 was parked just off the right side, halfway down the takeoff runway. As we taxied out in our Corsairs I could see Milway was standing on top of the PB4Y-2 pre-flighting his aircraft. Perfect! I couldn't resist. I took the right side of the runway for takeoff. I got airborne, picked up my gear, holding the Corsair down, blasting all 2,250 horsepower, right over the top of Milway. This was September 25, 1949. I wasn't to see Gene Milway again until I visited him on a motorcycle trip in 2003, 54 years later.

Firecrackers

The night before we were to leave for Pensacola for carrier qualifications, my roommates and I were feeling unusually jovial and carefree. We had successfully completed advanced

CHAPTER 4   ADVANCED TRAINING   81

training in the Corsair. I was cleaning out my dresser drawers and packing. Some new Midshipmen just checking in to the barracks stopped by our room to chat. As I came to the bottom of my dresser drawer, I found a package of firecrackers I'd forgotten. I offered the firecrackers to one of the new Midshipman. Before I could warn him about the restrictions to fireworks on the base, he ran out the back door, lit a firecracker and threw it into the night. Bang! The next thing I knew Marines were in our room, and we were braced against the wall. "OK, who threw that firecracker?!" As the Marines came to me I could honestly answer, "Not I Sir." "Were they your firecrackers?" I said, "No Sir." Of course, they used to be, but I had given them away.

On to Pensacola

In three months, we had become cocky fighter pilots. We had overcome our fear of the Corsair. The rigorous flying had built a strong camaraderie among us. Only one big hurdle lay between us and our goal of Golden Wings: Carrier Qualification in the Corsair.

The deaths of two of our shipmates in close order sobered us. Ensign Hugh Goodwin, son of Rear Admiral Hugh Goodwin, was killed in a mid-air collision at Cabaniss Field just before we departed. Shortly afterward, we got word of the death of another fellow Flying Midshipman in Carrier Qualifications at Corry Field, Pensacola. He had attempted a late wave off following a slower SNJ in the pattern. He rolled into a steep left bank while down adding full power. The great torque rolled the Corsair on its back. He hit the ground inverted and blew up.

Ensign Hugh Goodwin

I wondered how would I handle Carrier Qualifications? Did I have the guts?

I hitched a ride to Pensacola with Johnny Thompson and three other Midshipman. John

Kordeleski also drove his car with another load of Midshipmen. This was a much more enjoyable trip than my solo trip from Pensacola to Corpus Christi in my 1938 Plymouth.

We were full of ourselves, too full. Everyone in both cars had firecrackers. Each car would try to get in front and throw firecrackers out the window at the car behind. Thompson and Kordeleski started to play chicken, passing at the last minute so the car in back couldn't pass. There was a close call when Kordeleski almost didn't make it around a truck, just missing oncoming traffic. This scared us all. We agreed to be safe and get there in one piece.

Pensacola, here we come.

Chapter Five

Carrier Qualifications

Advanced Carrier Qualification

September 1949. I was back in Pensacola at Corry Field for the final phase of flight training, Advanced Carrier Qualifications or CQ. At this point it had been eighteen months of very intense, competitive flight training. We were the survivors of a system that was designed to weed out the weak or less talented, then mold aggressive naval aviators, future warriors.

We were self-assured twenty-one-year-olds brimming with confidence. We had just one more "big hill" to climb to get our Wings of Gold: Carrier Qualifications in the F4U-4 Corsair.

The Corsair had the worst accident record of any airplane in training or the fleet. Midshipmen with the best grades were assigned to train in the Corsair in attempt to keep accidents at an acceptable level. I took silent pride in being selected to fly the Corsair and looked forward to the challenge.

Chance Vought F4U-4 Corsair

Chapter 5   Carrier Qualifications

So far, I had done well, but CQ was the big test. I resolved early that I must not fail. I could not face the humiliation of going home without my wings. Still I knew Carrier Qualification in the Corsair would require all of the skill, courage and faith that I had in me.

Carrier Qualification, CQ or the CARQUAL phase, would be the most demanding training phase leading to our Navy Wings. This phase consisted of two segments, Field Carrier Landing Practice (FCLP) flown at an airfield marked as a carrier deck, and actual Carrier Landings on the light aircraft carrier, USS Cabot, CVL-28. Landing Signal Officers (LSOs) directed both segments of this phase.

FCLP consisted of three weeks of intense field carrier landing practice, usually flying two hops a day. Each flight or hop would require six to ten field carrier landings. Each landing was graded by the LSO. It took hundreds of field carrier landings to reach an acceptable level of proficiency.

We had to demonstrate that we could consistently fly the correct speed, altitude and alignment while instinctively following the LSO's commands. Only then we would be "Field Qualified," that is, be cleared to proceed to the Carrier Landing phase. Some of us qualified, and some did not.

A carrier deck was painted on Bronson Field near Perdido Bay for FCLP. Bronson was a wide macadam field without a real runway, about 15 miles from our home base at Corry Field, Pensacola. Before we began FCLP, we were given extensive briefings by the LSOs on the paddle signals, how to respond, the correct landing pattern altitudes and speeds, the communications procedures, etc.

Although we all knew the LSO signals, having previously qualified in the SNJ on the USS Wright months before, they were reviewed. Before our first FCLP, we were scheduled to fly the Corsair at slow speed at a safe altitude to explore the aircraft's characteristics. Mike Goodman and I took off together on this flight. At 5,000 feet, I practiced flying slower than the required 83 knots to get the feel of the carrier approach. It was spooky. I tried shallow turns at 78 to 80 knots, but it handled well enough if I was gentle on the controls.

I also explored the Corsair's torque roll tendency. I practiced

CHAPTER 5   CARRIER QUALIFICATIONS   85

rapidly adding full power with the left wing down, as it would be in a wave off, the maneuver that killed my friend. I found that I could control the Corsair's torque roll, only if I first leveled the wings to less than 20 degrees of bank before adding full power. If my left wing was down more than 30 degrees when full power was applied, full right rudder and aileron would not stop the roll, the Corsair would roll onto its back. I shared these experiences with Mike Goodman, Ned Steiner and others during our off hours. They shared similar experiences with me. We were losing some of the fear of the Corsair, even before we flew it low and slow.

Midshipman Dave Leue November F4U-4, Corry Field Pensacola

Twelve pilots were scheduled for FCLP at the same time. Of the twelve, six pilots would brief, man up and launch individually then fly to Bronson Field. The other six pilots would proceed to Bronson by bus.

Those flying to Bronson would make a low pass over the simulated carrier deck then make a sharp left turn, or "break," slow down the airplane, gear and flaps down, open and lock the canopy, mixture rich, prop low pitch, fly to the 180-degree position a half mile abeam the LSO at 200 feet altitude. At the 180, a left turn was begun slowing the airplane down to 85 knots, passing the 90-degree position the LSO was picked up in "the pocket" between the nose and the left wing. The pilot used throttle and nose attitude to maintain altitude and control speed. The LSO had control of the approach as soon as the pilot could see the signals. I tried to anticipate and fly at the correct speed, altitude and approach path, so all I would see was a "Roger"... the paddles outstretched horizontally.

CHAPTER 5 CARRIER QUALIFICATIONS

On my first FCLP pass, the first signal I saw was a "Come On," paddles coming together slowly, <u>you are slow</u>. I inched on a little power, flattened out, flew up and got a cut and landed. I immediately took off again for another pass.

This one pass gave a great boost to my confidence. I had worried that I wouldn't have the guts to fly the Corsair low and slow.

The consequences of making a mistake in a field carrier approach were intimidating. We had to fly the airplane just above the stall, or that point where your wings lost lift.

If we stalled the Corsair at low altitude, it would be fatal. It took intense concentration, skill and dexterity to fly just over the trees, with buffeting winds and turbulence, keeping track of the aircraft in front of me, finding the landmarks, picking up the LSO's signals, while maintaining altitude, attitude, line up and airspeed.

I was gaining confidence. Yet, I felt as if I was in over my head. My skills and courage were pushed to the limit. I prayed constantly.

Flying FCLP was so intense that after a period of six to ten landings the back of my flight suit, and indeed many times

Carrier Qualification Trivia Corry Field 1949

Chapter 5   Carrier Qualifications

my whole flight suit, would be wet with perspiration, even with the canopy open and a virtual tornado blowing through the cockpit.

We were debriefed after each flight by the LSO. Our LSO, LT "Lucky" Waller posted our grades in the LSO shack. A Roger (OK) pass was marked in green. I was working very hard, but I felt I was not doing well. However, when I checked, I had a lot of green on the board. Thank you, Lord!

Ned Steiner, Mike Goodman and I agreed, this was the most demanding thing we had done in our lives.

First Class Midshipman Ned Steiner

First Class Midshipman Ned Steiner

Upon entering the Carrier Qualification Phase at Pensacola we were all promoted to First Class Midshipmen. This was a big step. We were now allowed to use the Officer's Club, which was a big deal. Occasionally, after flying, Steiner and I would clean up and go to the club for "a cool one." We were almost officers, it felt good. Steiner introduced me to Heineken beer. I had never heard of Heineken. To this day, when I see Heineken, I think of Steiner. The challenges of flight training, but especially flying the Corsair in FCLP, had brought us very close together. We shared our common experiences, fears, goals and dreams. This bound us together like brothers.

Ned Steiner and I met at North Whiting Field in "A" Stage. He was a wonderful Catholic boy who didn't preach, but lived his faith. He came from Gary, Indiana. He had a happy enthusiasm for life that I admired. His favorite song was "Happy Talk" from the play "South Pacific." He talked eagerly about life and the aircraft he wanted to fly in the fleet. He taught me to play tennis and I taught him to sail in

CHAPTER 5   CARRIER QUALIFICATIONS   88

Pensacola Bay. He radiated a positive attitude about life that was a model for me. He helped me begin the process of dispelling the deep, private sadness that had followed me since my father's death.

Most of our buddies would go out drinking on Saturday nights. Steiner met and occasionally dated a Navy nurse from the base hospital. I was engaged to Jane, so I didn't date. Since neither Steiner nor I went to town, we were in shape to get up early Sunday, go to Mass, then see the town. I went to Mass with him to learn more about Jane's faith.

Steiner explained the Mass and the Church to me in a way that impressed me. He explained that Catholics believe Christ is present in the bread and wine at communion, that this was instituted by Christ at the Last Supper and had been carried on by the Apostles and their successors, priests for almost 2,000 years. Simple, direct. In time I came to believe this myself. It has been my rock.

In Field Carrier Landing Practice, Steiner qualified early and was scheduled to Carrier Qualify on USS Cabot several days ahead of me. Unfortunately, Steiner had trouble overshooting the groove on Cabot. In other words, he had trouble with the final line up on the carrier deck. This was not unusual. You could not see over a Corsair's nose and had to turn all the way to the "Cut." Also, the USS Cabot was a CVL or Light Carrier, built on a cruiser hull with a very narrow flight deck. Steiner was sent back for extra training.

On Steiner's first day of extra training, he was in the group of six pilots who flew to Bronson. He had taken off from Corry, flown his FCLP at Bronson and done well (I talked to the LSO later). He finished last, landed and taxied back and parked on the far right of a line of six Corsairs, all with engines running and idling over.

Steiner got out of his plane walking left in front of the line of whirling 14 foot Corsair props. He was probably deep in thought about his flight.

Meanwhile, Midshipman Rudy Krause, another fine Buffalo friend, eagerly manned his airplane, gave the pull chocks signal, added a blast of power to come out straight, then started a left clearing turn, as we were taught.

Chapter 5 — Carrier Qualifications 89

Flying Midshipman, Corry Field, 1949

Steiner was hidden under the long nose of Rudy's Corsair. Rudy's propeller killed Steiner instantly.

I was waiting to fly my second FCLP of the day in the Ready Room back at Corry at the time. I heard the crash alarm and the helicopter take off. Of course, there was nothing they could do. We were called into the Ready Room and told of the accident, who it was, and what had happened. In those days there was no such thing as a grief counselor. Thank God.

Later that day, as scheduled, I flew to Bronson, completed my FCLP, taxied by that terrible bloodstain on the macadam, said a prayer for Steiner, got out and went back to Corry on the bus. Back in the hangar, they had cleaned up Rudy Krause's Corsair. I ran my hand over the deeply scarred forged-aluminum propeller blade, and I said a another prayer for Ned Steiner.

The next day there was a solemn funeral Mass for Steiner. The young Catholic priest gave a wonderful homily. He spoke directly to all of Steiner's classmates. He said, "Don't fear. He is in heaven today. Have courage and do your duty." I took those words to heart, and I tried to follow in Steiner's footsteps.

Early on, I pondered how a loving God could take such a fine man, so young, so full of life, in such a brutal way. I have concluded that Steiner was a favored being, he went directly

CHAPTER 5   CARRIER QUALIFICATIONS   90

to heaven with no pain or suffering. He was spared the many terrors of years of battle that were to come, the repeated loss of brothers in arms, the temptations of success, the sorrows of failure and defeat, the stunning disappointments of an unbridled era and the slow relentless decline that comes with age.

However brief his life, Ned Steiner was a giant in my life, I thank God for him.

Two days after Steiner's death, I Field Qualified and was scheduled to go aboard USS Cabot the following day.

Carrier Qualifications, USS Cabot

November 9, 1949, was a sparkling, clear, blue Pensacola day. I took off and joined with three other Midshipmen on the wing of Lt "Lucky" Waller. We proceeded 20 miles south over the deep blue Gulf of Mexico. On arrival overhead, the USS Cabot began turning into the wind, leaving a sharply curving frothy white wake.

Our flight was given the "Charlie" signal. This meant we were cleared to land. Lt Waller put me on his right wing with the flight in right echelon. As we let down in a left turn, I could see the Cabot's white wake churning below. Coming up the stern and down the starboard side of the ship we leveled at 250 feet. Lt Waller passed the lead to me, then climbed to orbit overhead, waiting to lead us back to Pensacola.

In front of the bow I broke left over the sparkling Gulf. There were a few scattered white cumulus clouds overhead. I lowered my gear, opened the canopy, dropped landing flaps,

USS Cabot CVL–28

CHAPTER 5 CARRIER QUALIFICATIONS

opened the cowl flaps, mixture rich, prop low pitch and hook down. I went over my landing check list as I turned downwind.

I concentrated on keeping the Cabot in sight over my left shoulder. Passing the Cabot's island, going downwind, I put the stack on the horizon, as I had been taught. Abeam the ship's island I started my 180-degree turn toward the ship, dropping to 150 feet. I picked up the LSO passing the 90-degree position, easing down to 75 feet. I kept the LSO in the pocket between my left wing and nose, turning left toward the ship's wake. I made minor corrections responding to the LSO's signals, a slight high, a low dip, and the ship came rushing toward me. I received the "Cut."

I chopped the throttle, dropped my nose to view the deck, then tail down ... bam! On the center line, I was thrown into my shoulder straps.

F4U-4 Corsair Takes the "Cut"

I was aboard! A deck crewman off to my right immediately gave the "hook up" signal, his right thumb jammed into his open palm.

Hook up, power on, I taxi forward. Takeoff check list complete.

The Launching Officer, "Fly One," was standing to my right. He held up two fingers pointing down the deck. My signal for full throttle, I roared past the bridge, down the deck,

CHAPTER 5   CARRIER QUALIFICATIONS   92

New Naval Aviators, November 10, 1949

airborne, right clearing turn.

I completed seven landings within three quarters of hour, then joined LT Waller orbiting overhead, waiting as several others joined. We jubilantly returned to Corry Field.

We qualified!

The following day, November 10, 1949, we were officially presented our wings. Present were my good friends Midshipmen Mike Goodman, Ed Hofstra, Bob Wallin and Jim Radtke. I did not know a tall LT Bill Small, standing to my left. (Twenty-five years later, I would know him well. I would serve as Chief of Staff, for Rear Admiral Bill Small, Carrier Commander Carrier Group Three, USS Midway, Yokosuka, Japan).

Wings! A bittersweet day.

CHAPTER SIX

Fighter Squadron 24

Wings— Now what?

I had my Wings of Gold! How good it felt! I was a Naval Aviator, a First Class Midshipman with Wings! The Top. The realities of going from the Top (First Class Flying Midshipman with Wings in the Training Command), to the bottom (First Class Midshipman with Wings, in the Fleet), lower than an Ensign, were still to be discovered.

Leave

After two years of college and a year and a half of flight training, I was finally a Naval Aviator. I was on a high. This was the first real achievement in my life. Many of my buddies who had come with me from Buffalo, including the gent who predicted I would not make it, had quit or washed out and were sent home. Several had died in accidents. My good friends, Bob Wallin and Jim Radtke, received their wings at the same time as me. The three of us thumbed a ride to Eglin Air Force Base near Pensacola, then hitched a ride on a B-25 to Langley Field, Virginia. I won't ever forget that B-25 ride. It turned out to be the noisiest aircraft in the world, my ears rang for days afterward. From Langley Field, I hitched a ride home to Buffalo by truck to see Jane and my family. The battleship USS Missouri had recently run aground in Hampton Roads, Chesapeake Bay. The truck driver and I discussed the fate of the

Jane December 1949

CHAPTER 6   FIGHTER SQUADRON 24   94

Missouri's Captain, Navigator and Quartermaster as we travelled through the night.

Jane and I had a wonderful two weeks together. I was granted the use of a car, by a generous, well-to-do lady under my mother's care. Jane and I visited Niagara Falls and many of our old haunts. Things were looking up. Jane would complete her nurse's training within the year and then we could be married. We had been engaged for more than two years and we were ready. Really ready.

Naval Air Station, Oceana, Virginia

After leave, I returned to Oceana, Virginia, where Radtke, Wallin and I went to the Personnel Office of Commander Naval Air Forces, Atlantic, at Naval Air Station, Norfolk, for our squadron assignments. Our assignments were in the hands of a Lieutenant in the Personnel Office. He asked us where we wanted to be assigned. We all responded that we wanted to go to Fighter Squadron 23 at NAS Oceana. That's where most of our buddies, Jim Brogan, "Buck" Bustard, Jack Brinkley and George Sinkez had been assigned. The Personnel Officer responded, "Why do you guys all want to be Fighter Pilots? I need TBM (torpedo) pilots, how'd you like to go a Torpedo Squadron?" We pleaded, "No, no, not a torpedo squadron, please!" He had mercy on us and sent us to a sister squadron at NAS Oceana, Attack Squadron 24, also flying Corsairs. He told us, "Within a month, Attack

 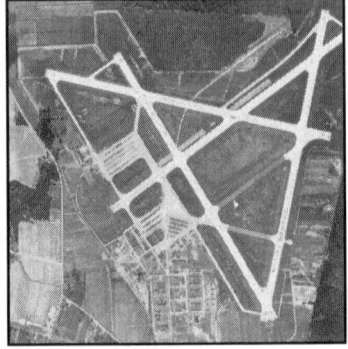

NAS Oceana 1949

CHAPTER 6   FIGHTER SQUADRON 24

Squadron 24 will be re-designated Fighter Squadron Twenty-Four." We were now fighter pilots in the Atlantic Fleet! Fighter Squadron-Twenty Four would prove to be the very best squadron.

Fighter Squadron Twenty Four

Fighter Squadron Twenty-Four (VF-24) was based at Naval Air Station Oceana, Virginia, located in Virginia Beach about ten miles east of Norfolk. The squadron consisted of eighteen F4U-4 Corsairs, twenty-four officers and roughly 150 enlisted men. It was part of Carrier Air Group Two, which had four Corsair squadrons and one Skyraider (AD) squadron. This Air Group was nominally assigned to the carrier USS Midway, hence, the "M" on all of its aircraft tails. Naval Air Station Oceana, Virginia, had only very basic facilities at that time. VF-24's airplanes were parked in the open, on interlocking steel matting, Marsten Mat, of WWII fame. The Ready Room was a wooden frame hut with a pot-bellied stove. We had no hangar or proper office spaces. Maintenance was performed in the open, summer or winter. Oceana Naval Air Station reflected the realties of the times. World War II had been over just four years. The country believed there would never be another war, the military budget reflected this belief.

A friendly steward's mate, Melvin, kept the pot-bellied stove stoked with coal on the cold December and January mornings. The pilots were a mixture of a few World War II aviators and many, like myself, Midshipmen with brand new Wings, just out of flight training. The squadron personnel reflected the post WWII austerity. The squadron had two Lieutenant Commanders, two Lieutenants, two Lieutenants Junior Grade and the rest of us were Midshipmen or Ensigns.

VF-24 Ready Room NAS Oceana

CHAPTER 6 FIGHTER SQUADRON 24

VF-24 Corsairs NAS Oceana

Our Commanding Officer, or Skipper, was Lieutenant Commander Emery R. Coffman. He was a tall, well-built southern man, a Catholic, who had played football for Alabama in the Rose Bowl. He was a natural leader and greatly respected in the squadron. Our Executive Officer (XO) was Lieutenant Commander Bill Matthews. He had limited fighter experience. His background was primarily in multi-engine flying boats. LCDR Matthews had a pleasant, easy- going southern manner. I was assigned to fly his wing. I was also assigned as Assistant Flight Officer in the Operations Department. My job was to assist the Flight Officer in his duties of making out the training plan, flight schedules and record keeping.

The Operations Officer (OPS) was Lieutenant Skip Hendricks. The Operations Officer is the third most senior officer in the squadron, under the Commanding Officer and Executive Officer. In a Navy squadron, all aviators, in addition to their flying duties, have administrative duties. Under the Commanding Officer, Executive Officer and Operations Officer, there are the Maintenance Officer, the Administrative Officer, the Intelligence Officer and the Supply Officer and their assistants. In some squadrons, the maintenance and supply duties may be shared with non-flying officers.

LCDR Matthews, ENS Elmore

I quickly fell into the routine of a Fleet squadron. We were training

CHAPTER 6   FIGHTER SQUADRON 24

in preparation for a deployment on the USS Coral Sea to the Mediterranean in about four months. We flew daily training missions practicing navigation, formation, aerial gunnery, dive bombing and strafing. On most of my missions I flew on LCDR Matthew's wing. There was strong, friendly competition among our four-plane division and other divisions in our bombing rocket and strafing scores.

Skipper, LCDR Coffman 1950

We were encouraged to fly cross-country flights on weekends to gain proficiency in navigation, map reading and general flying skills.

Although I had my wings, I realized how much I still had to learn to be a professional, productive Naval officer and fighter pilot, both administratively and in the air. I tried to keep my mouth shut, listen and learn. It soon became apparent that the Skipper Coffman, XO Mathews and OPS Hendricks were an outstanding leadership team. They led primarily by example, keeping their voices and the tension level low. They were tolerant of our inexperience, except where safety was involved, which made the young Midshipmen feel like an important part of the team. Morale was high.

Aerial Gunnery Competition

VF-24 was scheduled for an Operational, Administrative and Material inspection in March 1950. This inspection included competition in aerial gunnery. This gunnery competition would be held at 15,000 feet, shooting at a 6-foot-by-20-foot banner target, towed 500 feet behind another Corsair. The firing would be conducted in restricted areas over the Atlantic Ocean. Flights of four Corsairs would rendezvous

Chapter 6   Fighter Squadron 24

VF-24 Pilots check hits during competition 1950

with the tow plane then climb to 18,000 feet, parallel with and 3,000 feet above the tow plane. Each pilot would peel off, one at a time, rollover and dive straight down on the target. The Corsair had six 50-caliber machine guns, three in each wing. Each gun held 400 rounds of ammunition. In the competition, we would fire only two guns, one in each wing. The Corsair had to be flown in a vertical dive to a point 800 feet above the target. The pilot had to fire with the correct lead, or distance in front of the target, for a brief second, then pull out of the screaming dive, pull up and do this again, until he had expended 100 rounds in each of two wing guns. Our guns were sited to converge 800 feet in front of the airplane. This maneuver was called an "Overhead Gunnery Run."

I had never practiced Overhead Runs in training. Before the competition, I was fortunate to fly wing on Lieutenant Tom Hoskins, an experienced fighter pilot. Tom showed me the proper distance to start my turn abeam and how to hold the Corsair inverted briefly before the dive, in order to get the correct sight picture in the Overhead Run.

We had only two training flights before the competition. With Lieutenant Hoskin's help, I caught on quickly.

CHAPTER 6   FIGHTER SQUADRON 24

To separate our hits on the banner, our ordnance crews dipped each pilot's bullet tips in a different color of paint.

In the competition on March 6, 1950, I flew LT Hoskin's wing again. It was a beautiful clear day. Everything went perfectly. My guns fired flawlessly, they were bore-sited perfectly and my runs and aim were right on. When they counted the hits in the target banner I had 40 hits out of my 200 rounds! The Navy "E" for Excellence, required 10% hits. I had shot 20%. It was a very proud moment for me. I was still a Midshipman, with a Navy "E" for gunnery painted on my airplane.

Administrative and Material Inspection (ADMAT)

The purpose of the ADMAT inspection was to determine if the squadron was complying with Navy rules and regulations. We were closely examined by inspectors as to our administrative procedures. Although I was the most junior officer in the squadron I had been assigned the collateral duty of Safety Officer. Safety was apparently not a high priority in Naval aviation at that time, aircraft were cheap and the bravado of World War II aviators was still strong.

Crawford, Wallin, Leue' & Motley

On the morning of the inspection, I was very nervous. I had gone over the administrative check sheet for Safety many times, but I was still unsure of myself. The inspector sat down at the Operations Officer's desk, I stood at his right looking over his shoulder, waiting for his questions. LT Skip Hendricks, our Operations officer, stood directly in back of me. Looking over the inspector's shoulder I noticed he had a new check sheet! The first question was, "Who is the safety officer?" The second question was, "Is he a <u>senior</u> officer in the squadron?" Obviously, I wasn't a senior officer.

The inspector asked, "Who is the safety officer?" I opened my mouth to say, "I am, Sir!" However, LT Hendricks, apparently seeing the second question, quickly covered my mouth with his hand. He stepped forward and said, "I am Sir, LT Hendricks." He went through the check sheet and apparently satisfactorily answered the questions, because with our gunnery scores, the squadron received the overall Navy "E" for the outstanding Fighter Squadron in the Atlantic Fleet for 1950!

In the spring of 1950, in preparation for a deployment on the USS Coral Sea to the Mediterranean, we continued our gunnery, dive bombing, formation and strafing training. We were again encouraged to take cross-countries to other cities on the weekends to build our flight time and gain experience.

Cross Country to Miami

Miami, March 12, 1950

On March 10, 1950, Skipper, LCDR Coffman, led an unforgettable cross-country flight. Previously, the Skipper happened to mention that he would to fly to Miami Beach to see Sam Snead play in the U.S. Open, would anybody care to accompany him? Two-thirds of the squadron volunteered to go with him! It was a fun trip. We flew nonstop, 4.7 hours, from NAS Oceana, Virginia, to Opa Loka, Florida, near Miami Beach. Of course, we acted like fighter pilots on liberty. I can remember paying the outrageous price of one dollar for a beer at a strip-tease joint and eating lobster for the first time. Miami Beach was the most opulent and splendid city I had ever seen.

Chapter 6   Fighter Squadron 24

Operation Swarmer

In April 1950, the Air Group participated in an operation with the Air Force called "Swarmer." In this operation, we flew simulated close air support missions in and around Pope Air Force Base in North Carolina. On one memorable Swarmer mission, I flew on the wing of LT Bernie Levi. LT Levi led us from our base at NAS Oceana down to North Carolina, where we conducted a simulated close air support mission with a ground controller. During our close air support mission we were jumped by four Air Force F-84 jet fighters from the "Orange" forces.

Levi, Leue', Matthews, Sundstrom

LT Levi called the F-84s position to me, then turned hard toward the inside of the F84's circle of turn, keeping their guns off of us, then at the last minute, he reversed hard back toward them. Now we had them in our sights.

I learned a valuable lesson that day from LT Bernie Levi. If a faster fighter, such as a jet fighter, tries to attack a more maneuverable fighter, the more maneuverable fighter can defeat the fast attacker, if he is clever. I used this tactic many times flying a Corsair in mock battles with friendly jets. If they wanted to play, I would sucker them in, like LT Levi did, then turn hard into them and defeat them. Of course, if they didn't want to fight, there was nothing I could do about it. This was the essential tactic taught years later in "Top Gun."

I also learned another valuable lesson that day on Bernie Levi's wing: When he reversed unexpectedly back toward those attacking jets, I almost ran into him. I was looking at the jets, instead of at my leader. A wingman must never lose sight of his leader, not for an instant.

CHAPTER 6 FIGHTER SQUADRON 24

Life in the Oceana BOQ

The Oceana Bachelors Officers Quarters were hastily built, early World War II vintage two-story, wood-construction barracks, that needed paint. They reflected the condition of the entire base. Drab. However, the BOQ was populated by an eclectic group of twenty-something Naval Aviators, all characters. Most of the squadron pilots were unmarried and lived in the BOQ. A few bachelors banded together to rent places in town, usually called "Snake Ranches" for the parties they claimed took place there.

Acey Ducey VF-24 Ready Room

No females were allowed in the BOQ. Most of us in the BOQ were saving our money and planning for the future. Jim Radtke, Bob Wallin, Sandy Sunstrom, Bill Warwick and myself were going with women we hoped to marry. Bill Hugo, Keith Knott and several others in VF-24 also lived in the BOQ. We all ate in the general mess, since the Officer's Club did not serve meals. The Officer's Club did have a bar with a black and white TV, which was open in the evenings. Wallin and Radtke spent a lot of time at the bar. Sunstrom almost never drank, but he never missed the "Kukla, Fran and Olli" show on TV.

Hugo took up painting in acrylics. He did two paintings that he was proud of and put them up in his room. One was titled "Babylonian Ziggurats in the Morning." This painting was of tall black and dark grey rocks with long blue-black shadows. It was quite good, I thought. Radtke, coming back from the bar one evening, had other thoughts. Apparently, Hugo's artistic pretentiousness was too much for Radtke. A day later, Radtke finished his own painting and put it up in his

CHAPTER 6   FIGHTER SQUADRON 24

room. It was dark brown mounds with long shadows, entitled, "A Batch of Crap at Sunset."

Sunstrom, we called him Sandy, purchased a WWII trainer, a BT-13, for $500.00. He recovered the rudder and elevators fabric in his room in the BOQ. The fumes from the acetate dope he used were overwhelming. We complained, but he persisted. I helped Sandy on this job and he rewarded me by taking me flying one Sunday. The BT-13 was similar to the SNJ. It had fore and aft seating, but with fixed landing gear. I sat in the back and we flew out to a small abandoned field south of Oceana, Fentress Field. Sandy made a landing, then asked me, "Do you want fly it?" I said, "Sure!" and we switched places. I checked the gas gauges and both indicated "Empty." I said, "Sandy, there's no gas in this airplane!" He said, "Don't worry, they indicate low, we have enough to get back to Virginia Beach Airport." I said, "OK, it's your airplane." I took off and we made it to Virginia Beach Airport.

Sandy was not always so lucky. He flew his BT-13 to New York on weekends to see his girlfriend. On these flights, Sandy would carry two sailors in the back for $50 each, to pay for his gas. On his last trip, just before we departed for Korea, he came back late at night. He tried to at land at the little Virginia Beach Airport, which had no lights. He ran off the end of the runway, nosing it up on the railroad tracks. The squadron left the next day for Korea. He left the BT-13 on the railroad tracks!

Evenings in our BOQ I read or wrote letters to pass the time. I read an electronics magazine that described how to build a two-tube, regenerative radio receiver. One Saturday, I took the bus into Norfolk, purchased the required supplies and proceeded to construct my radio. It had no speaker, just ear-phones. To my surprise it worked quite well with only one

Dave's home made radio

problem. If I turned the volume too high, it would transmit a squeal through-out all the radios in the BOQ. Bob Wallin found out I was the source of this outrage. Anytime I turned the volume too high, I could be sure Wallin would storm into my room with fire in his eyes. Ah, life in the BOQ.

Commissioned Ensign

Ensign Leue'

On June 1, 1950, I was commissioned an Ensign in the United States Regular Navy. It had been four years since I joined the Navy as an Apprentice Seaman, then a senior in Buffalo Technical High School, Buffalo, New York. Now I was free to marry Jane. I, like most of my Midshipmen buddies, had declined a Reserve Commission six months earlier because we wanted to be Regular Navy, not Reserve.

Naval Gunfire Spot Training

LCDR Matthews, my Executive Officer, called me into his office in early June to congratulate me on my commissioning as Ensign. While I was in his office he said, "Dave, how would you like to go to school?" The only school I knew of, open to fleet pilots, was the All Weather Flight School in Key West, Florida. I said, "Great, I'd love to go, Sir." He said, "Good, I'm sending you to Gunfire Spotting School in Little Creek, Virginia. It starts next Monday." I was disappointed. I felt Naval Gunfire Spotting was below a fighter pilot's dignity. However, orders were orders. I reported for training at Little Creek the following Monday.

The course was excellent. They explained the capabilities and the limitations of naval gunfire from 5-inch guns to 16-inch guns and everything in between. I still have the notebook that I kept during my training. Once we mastered the basics, we trained on a realistic terrain board set up in a large auditorium. We sat in seats high above the terrain board, as if we were in an aircraft. The terrain board simulated a coastal area with hills, roads, railroads, towns and military

CHAPTER 6 FIGHTER SQUADRON 24

Ensign Dave Leue' June 23, 1950 Bloodsworth Island

installations. With this terrain board, they could simulate a ship bombarding targets ashore. Little smoke puffs would emerge from the position that we directed our naval gunfire.

Once we had mastered this phase of our training we were scheduled to fly and direct actual gunfire of destroyers at an impact range in the Chesapeake Bay called Bloodsworth Island. On June 13, 1950 at Bloodsworth Island impact range, I directed the 5-inch guns of a Navy destroyer, passing the course, and was certified to direct the gunfire of Naval warships up to and including the 16-inch guns of battleships. This training would prove to be invaluable to me after we deployed to Korea later in the year.

The Air Force had sent several F-80 jet pilots to train as naval gunfire spotters with us. These F-80 pilots were scheduled at Bloodsworth Island immediately following me. As I was returning to Oceana at about 10,000 feet, I noticed the two F-80s cruising by about 2,000 feet below me. I rolled in, picking up speed to attack them in mock combat. They pulled into a loop trying to shake me. They made the mistake of continuing to turn with me instead of diving away. I firewalled the Corsair. At full power I had enough performance to stay right with the turning F-80s. No matter what they tried, I was right there at their "six." This gave me great confidence that if an enemy jet pilot, such as a Mig, tried to turn with me, I could kill him.

Chapter 6 Fighter Squadron 24

The next day I saw these F-80 pilots and they said to me, "Boy, I'll bet you had one burned-out Corsair." I smiled and said, "No strain."

June 25, 1950, Korean War Begins

As I gained more experience, I became qualified to lead more junior pilots on cross-countries. Midshipman Clayton Roland Robinson, a local Norfolk boy, had joined our squadron and asked me if I would lead him to Jacksonville in early June. I agreed on the condition that he'd accompany me to Buffalo later. Regulations required we have a wingman. I led Roland Robinson to Jacksonville on June 23, 1950. We flew back from Jacksonville on Sunday, June 25, 1950. On return to NAS Oceana, I roared over the runway with Robinson on my right wing at well over 200 knots, broke left with my Corsair, pulling five Gees in a very tight left turn, with vapor coming off my wing tips, showing off, then lowering my landing gear and landing.

After I landed, I noticed the entire squadron was busy loading ammunition, as if preparing for war. I taxied into our line, jumped out and spoke to a squadron Second Class Ordnance man named Kusic, who I knew from Buffalo. I said, "Kusic, what's going on? It looks like we are at war." He said, "Sir, where have you been? We are at war!" I said, 'Where?' He said, 'Korea.' I am ashamed to say I wasn't sure where Korea was located. I thought of French Indochina. I would find out soon enough.

Korean War Briefing

The next morning, June 26, 1950, Lieutenant Commander Coffman gathered the squadron in the Ready Room. He briefed us on the war situation in Korea. He said the North Koreans had attacked the South Koreans across the Demilitarized Zone (DMZ) and were pushing south through the capital of Seoul. He told us not to worry, Air Group Two had extra squadrons. Our Air Group would not fit on the smaller Pacific Fleet Essex class aircraft carriers. The Skipper told us he was certain, we would deploy to the Mediterranean

CHAPTER 6 FIGHTER SQUADRON 24

in two months, aboard the USS Coral Sea, as scheduled. This was good news. Jane and I could be married soon.

All Propeller, Air Group Two

The war in Korea turned ugly, very quickly. North Korean troops, with Russian T-34 tanks, were over-running South Korean and American troops. All the airfields in South Korea were overrun. U.S. Air Force planes had to fly all the way from Japan, making them ineffective. The call went out for Navy aircraft carriers, with Navy propeller fighter aircraft, capable of providing close air support. They did not want jet aircraft. They wanted Navy propeller fighters and attack aircraft that could carry heavy bombs and stay on station. Carrier Air Group Two had four fighter and one attack squadron. Unfortunately, two of our Fighter Squadrons, VF-21 and VF-22, were transitioning into F9F-2 jet aircraft at that time. Only Fighter Squadron 24 and Fighter Squadron 23 had Corsair propeller fighters. To make up an all propeller Air Group the Navy combined Fighter Squadrons 23 and 24 with Fighter Squadrons 63 and 64 flying Corsairs, and Attack Squadron 65, flying AD Skyraiders, from Air Group Six. This new organization was called Air Group Two. Commander Don White was designated the Commander Air Group (CAG).

In July, we were told Air Group Two would fly to the West Coast, board the USS Boxer then deploy to Korea.

To Buffalo

Jane, Niagara Falls

I asked permission to make one last cross country, to see Jane. This was granted. On July 22, 1950, flying Corsairs, I led Midshipman Robinson through a clear, blue sky for two hours, landing at Niagara Falls Naval Air Station. We stayed with Jane's parents in Buffalo. We visited briefly with my sister, Dolly, and brother-in-law, Speas, and my mother, who was working as a nurse taking care of an older couple on the shore of Lake Erie. In June, I had

CHAPTER 6   FIGHTER SQUADRON 24

assured Jane that our Skipper had told us we would not go to Korea, but now I had to tell her we had been ordered to Korea. We would have to delay our wedding plans. I stayed only one day but it was a great visit.

On July 23, 1950, we departed Naval Air Station Niagara Falls, my sister and brother-in-law, Jane and her mother and father all came to watch our takeoff. Robbie and I took off, roaring low over the families' heads as they stood at the end of the runway. I asked the tower to make a low pass, which was granted. We again blasted over their heads, at full throttle. Here was the skinny hometown kid, flying a Navy Corsair! It was big moment for me. We went off into the wild blue and flew along the coast of Lake Erie. I found where my mother was working. She came out and waved. We made a low pass down the beach, just over her head. I would not see Jane or the family again for almost a year.

Refresher-Training in Carrier Landings

USS Coral Sea CVB 43

On July 26th we flew out to USS Saipan, where the squadron practiced carrier landings. I logged six carrier landings. This was followed by an intense week at sea on USS Coral Sea, where we conducted weapons training and I logged another ten carrier landings.

To California—Lost in a Storm

In August, preparations were made to transport the crew and equipment by train to Alameda, California. The eighteen planes of Fighter Squadron 24 would fly first to Dallas, Texas, then to Alameda, California, in two flights. Only the

Chapter 6   Fighter Squadron 24

eighteen most senior pilots would fly. I was number eighteen.

Early on the morning of August 14, 1950, we took off from Oceana, Virginia, into a misty unsettled sky. I took off last, number eighteen, flying on LT Hoskins wing. We always flew in divisions of four, so Hoskins and I were the extra section. Hoskins and I flew as five and six in Skipper Coffman's division. This made me number five down a right echelon. This was not problem, until we encountered a cold front.

Skipper Coffman filed a flight plan and plunged into the storm front with all eighteen aircraft flying formation. We flew into severe turbulence. Since I was at the end of a five-plane echelon the turbulence made me go up and down like a whip. Visibility was so poor I had to fly very close just to see Hoskin's aircraft. I almost collided with Tom Hoskins.

The turbulence continued, after just missing a collision with Hoskins a second time, I broke away. The next moment, we flew into a clearing. I whipped around and tried to rejoin Hoskin's wing. Instantly, we flew back into the clouds. I strained to see Hoskin's aircraft looking intently out my windscreen. Not watching my instruments, my Corsair rolled onto its back.

I heard my speed building rapidly in a screaming dive.

My training kicked in. I went to my instruments. I centered the turn needle rolling up right, let my nose come up, then climbed to regain my altitude. I climbed higher, putting on my oxygen mask, putting the engine into high blower (supercharger), topping the overcast at about 25,000 feet. Listening to the radio, I could tell that many had broken out of the formation. Now the squadron was scattered all over everywhere.

Skipper Coffman radioed that all would rejoin on the other side of the cold front, at Montgomery, Alabama. I tried to navigate above the overcast with the only navigation radio we had in a Corsair. This was a low-frequency receiver used to follow the old Adcock AM radio ranges. I tried to listen for

CHAPTER 6   FIGHTER SQUADRON 24   110

an "A" (dit-da) or an N (da-dit) and then get on the beam. The front created so much static, however, I could not hear my range receiver. I just flew a dead-reckoning course, keeping track of roughly where I was on a chart I had plenty of gas and charts for the whole United States, so I wasn't too worried.

I finally came to a hole on the other side of the cold front. I put my gear down, as speed brakes, spiraled down through the hole and got underneath the overcast. I was not sure where I was. I went down low and tried to read signs. I found a small airport and tried to read the name on the runway, but no luck. Finally, I found a barn with the latitude and longitude painted on the roof! These signs had been used during the 1920s and 1930s, by early aviators. Just a few weeks before in the BOQ, Sandy Sundstrom, was looking at old CAA documents on this procedure, "How to make latitude and longitude paintings on a barn." I laughed and said, "That's stupid. Who cares about that nowadays?" Boy, was I wrong.

I broke out my chart, put a big X at my latitude and longitude, drew a course to Montgomery Alabama, and pushed the throttle up to the maximum continuous power: manifold pressure 46 inches of Mercury and 2,600 rpm. I was the second of eighteen planes to arrive at Montgomery, Alabama.

We refueled, then flew to Dallas, Texas, without incident. Chance Vaught Aircraft, makers of the Corsair, threw a big

Air Group Two Corsairs fly over Chance Vought, Dallas August 15, 1950

CHAPTER 6   FIGHTER SQUADRON 24   111

party for Air Group Two that night. In the morning, we flew nonstop to NAS Los Alamitos in Los Angeles, a flight of seven hours non-stop. The Corsair had the world's most uncomfortable seat. My butt hurt.

After we refueled, we flew on to NAS Alameda. The next day our aircraft were loaded aboard USS Boxer and, shortly

USS Boxer CV-21

thereafter we departed for Korea.

The USS Boxer was a World War II Essex class aircraft carrier. Junior officers were assigned to bunk rooms. I was assigned to one of the smaller bunk rooms, with twelve men. Jim Radtke and Jim Brogan were also assigned to that bunk room. The bunks were stacked three high with little space in between. There was very little space to store things and you had to be able to get along with people at close quarters. I actually, enjoyed the environment.

VF-24 Pilots flight deck USS Boxer

The Squadron's operational center of gravity was the Ready Room. Each Squadron had its own Ready Room and each pilot had an assigned seat.

Chapter 6 Fighter Squadron 24

As we crossed the vast Pacific Ocean, we conducted daily training on weapons and tactics. Intelligence officers briefed us on the latest situation in Korea.

We stopped briefly in Hawaii and conducted weapons training on targets in that area. We dropped our first live weapons on the island of Kaneohe. The ship pulled into Pearl Harbor for a day of liberty. We had a great Air Group Two party at Don the Beachcombers. It probably was a little too great, because for the next six months, the Air Group got bills to repair the damage done to Don the Beachcombers.

Don the Beachcomber's dancer enthralls Radtke, Warwick ,Sunstrom & Brogan

Ensign Zimmerly VF-63

Ensign Art Zimmerly of VF-63 became quite famous at this point. He woke up very late in the morning after the party. The ship had already departed. Zimmerly went to the Naval Air Station and caught a ride on a helicopter out to the Boxer. When the helicopter arrived the Boxer's skipper, Captain Camron Briggs, ordered "Side Boys," on the flight deck, to render honors, thinking a VIP was coming aboard. Ensign Zimmerly emerged to be awarded two weeks in "Hack" (confined to his room). Thank you, Captain! If

Chapter 6   Fighter Squadron 24

Zimmerly had missed the ship completely, he would have been court-martialed.

Shortly, the USS Boxer, CVA-21, with Carrier Air Group Two, headed west at flank speed toward Korea. Chapter I covers our adventures on that first brief combat cruise. The following chapter picks up the story as we returned triumphantly to the USA on the USS Boxer.

CHAPTER SEVEN

USS Valley Forge
Home are the Heroes

USS BOXER passes under the Bay bridge, November 17, 1950

Returning from Korea, USS Boxer entered San Francisco harbor November 15, 1950. Air Group Two was put ashore at NAS Alameda, California. We were billeted in the substantial NAS Alameda Bachelor Officers Quarters (BOQ). It was a palace compared to NAS Oceana BOQ or the USS Boxer bunkroom. I was excited about taking leave and marriage to Jane. However, there were still unforeseen bumps in the road.

Dear John (Dave)

I felt good about my decision to become a Catholic, however, it was far from a decision that was free of controversy. My mother, a daughter of a Lutheran minister, was not pleased.

Chapter 7   USS Valley Forge   115

Similarly, Jane's stepmother, also Protestant, with similar views of Catholics, was dismayed. I received letters from both. They were very blunt advising me that it would be unwise for Jane and I to marry under Catholic doctrine.

I told them in a nice way that it was none of their business. However, Vera had great influence over Jane, and before long I received a letter from Jane, saying in effect, that she couldn't marry me under these conditions. There was an exchange of letters and phone calls, which culminated with Jane saying, "The wedding is off." She said she would send back the ring. We had been engaged and written every day for almost three years, but now communications broke down completely.

My life fell apart.

Off to San Diego

I was feeling quite low, my whole life had fallen to pieces at once. About this time, the Squadron Duty Officer (SDO) inquired if anyone wanted go to San Diego to pick up some Corsairs. I volunteered. I wanted to get out of town. Four of us were flown south to San Diego in a twin Beechcraft to pick up the Corsairs. Since I only planned on being gone one day, I had packed only my aviation greens uniform, some underwear and about $10. Flying back, we ran into the San Joaquin Valley fog. The one-day trip lasted six days, five of them in Bakersfield. I went out with the boys for the first time in three years and met a gal, and got rid of some of my gloom. We were returning heroes, right?

Big Hairy Dog Fight

About two days later, I was scheduled for a routine training flight with Ensign Bill Sheehy as my wingman flying out of NAS Alameda. It was a bright beautiful day. We took off climbing south over the Bay, past Hayward Field. Two Air National Guard, F-51, Mustang fighters from Hayward jumped us.

The fight was on. No one did that to Navy fighter pilots. I went to full power, turned into the first F-51 and quickly maneuvered to his six o'clock. I was surprised, my Corsair's 2,250 horsepower Pratt Whitney R-2800, had no problem at all staying with the Mustang. He did everything he could to shake me, loops, rolls, high Gee barrel rolls, reversals, you name it. He couldn't shake me. My Corsair could out-turn, out-climb and out-run the F-51.

I was thrilled. I knew what a great fighter the Mustang was. Now it just seemed so easy to take him. We were fighting right through the San Francisco Bay Airways. Strictly illegal, and very dangerous, but I just couldn't let this challenge go. I followed the Mustang as he went through every acrobatic maneuver. We went by airliners on our backs.

F-51 Mustang

In the middle of this fight, Bill Sheehy inexplicably broke off from his fight with the other Mustang, and made a pass at my Mustang. He didn't see me a hundred yards to the rear. He roared by me, in a vertical bank, so close, I felt him go by.

Just a foot or two in either direction and we would have both been history.

I continued to ease up closer on my Mustang joining on his right wing. Finally, low on fuel he returned to Hayward Field, his home base. I stayed very tight on his right wing, my prop just off his wing tip. When he broke to land over Hayward Field, I broke with him, then returned to Alameda.

Our dog fighting was strictly against the rules, especially in the Bay Area near civilian traffic. I compounded the felony by going into the Hayward pattern tight on the F-51's wing. I was very excited about whipping the Mustang. I was also very apprehensive about being put on report.

Chapter 7   USS Valley Forge

Back to War

I landed, then hurried up to the second deck of our Alameda hangar, to our Ready Room. Ensign Bob Wallin was the Squadron Duty Officer. As I entered the Ready Room, Wallin called, "Hey, Louie, (my nick-name) did you hear what happened?"

I was petrified. I knew I'd been put on report. I said, "No, what happened?"

He said, "Air Group Two is going back to Korea! We have just three days to board the USS Valley Forge in San Diego and depart for Korea. The Chinese have entered the war. Our troops are being overrun. They need us now."

I was relieved. I wasn't on report! In truth, I wanted to go back into combat. I had nothing to lose, after all, Jane had said goodbye, and I was spoiling for a real fight.

USS Valley Forge

When USS Boxer and Air Group Two departed for the USA in October 1950, the North Korean Army had been defeated. U.S. and U.N. forces had advanced to the Yalu River, unifying Korea. In late November, without warning and without provocation, Chinese armies crossed the Yalu River into North Korea, surrounding and cutting off U.S. and U.N. forces.

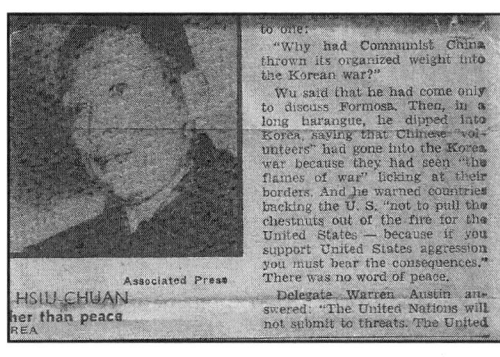

Buffalo Evening News December 1950

Our troops were overwhelmed by the sheer numbers of Chinese troops. They were fighting for their lives in the frozen mountains of North Korea. They needed all the Navy air support they could get, right now! Air Group Two, trained and ready in Alameda, California, was immediately ordered back to Korea. Our ship, the USS Boxer, was in the shipyard

CHAPTER 7 USS VALLEY FORGE

being repaired. Now, we were ordered to immediately board the USS Valley Forge in San Diego.

On December 2, 1950, Air Group Two flew by squadrons from NAS Alameda, California, to NAS North Island, San Diego, California. After landing, we taxied directly from the Naval Air Station, North Island, down a wide boulevard, directly to the pier. We were loaded on board the USS Valley Forge (CV-45), by the ship's crane.

USS Valley Forge had recently returned from a full Korean deployment of more than six months. It was quickly readied for redeployment.

There must have been many surprised and disappointed sailors on the USS Valley Forge. However, Valley Forge was a very good ship, and the crew quickly overcame their disappointment, and turned to the task of getting Air Group Two aboard. USS Valley Forge (CV-45), was an Essex class carrier, the same class as USS Boxer (CV-21), but was newer, cleaner and in better shape. It deserved the moniker, "Happy Valley."

This amazing turn of events took my mind off my own troubles. I busied myself helping get the squadron operations gear aboard, helping the crew get berthed, and getting my personal gear aboard ship. I put my personal troubles away. This was a big adventure, our troops in Korea needed us. I was excited.

I was berthed in the Junior Officer's bunkroom, "Boys Town," which was just forward of the hanger deck and aft of the Forecastle. This was a step down from the twelve man bunkroom of the Boxer. This JO bunkroom, had forty-two bunks. The bunks were three high, stacked next to one another. I just had a small part of a locker to hang uniforms, a drawer for incidentals, such as skivvies, and not much else. There were about eight to ten stainless-steel sinks in the entire bunk room, with three round poker type tables, and a total of maybe twelve chairs. The "head" was aft down the passageway.

Chapter 7   USS Valley Forge   119

Every night in the bunkroom, there were several card games and three or four 45 rpm records, playing at the same time. The catapults ran just outboard of the bunkroom on either side. When the cats fired, it sounded like a freight train going through the bunkroom at high speed. Amazingly, I actually enjoyed the happy din, and could go to sleep whenever I wanted to, no problem. I usually wrote letters, then read myself to sleep.

Heading back across the wide Pacific my thoughts differed from those on Boxer a few months before. Now, I had a feeling of what combat was like. I knew there would be risks from anti-aircraft guns, enemy aircraft, weather and high-tempo carrier operations. I was now more confident in my training and abilities. In our cruise on the Boxer, we had lost aircraft and friends from flak and accidents, but now, at least I knew the risks, and I felt that I could cope with them. I looked forward to the challenge. I had a strong faith and I was ready to die if necessary. The Air Group as a whole was much more professional than a few months ago.

Great News

Passing the Hawaiian Islands, mail was flown aboard and I received a wonderful letter from Jane. She had changed her mind! What good news! We would be married when I returned. The date was totally uncertain, because no one in the Navy had any idea when we would be home.

Dave smiles after getting great news from home

CHAPTER 7 USS VALLEY FORGE 120

VF–63 Ready Room USS Valley Forge heading back to Korea December 1950

Our troops in Korea were taking a terrible licking. Our first priority was to get there fast and stay as long as needed to support them. The Essex class carriers were fast ships. The Valley Forge, with a brief stop in Hawaii, averaged 25 knots for the crossing.

We flew training flights approaching Korea on December 20, 1950. Shortly, USS Valley Forge joined Task Force 77, this time, operating about one hundred miles east of Korea, in the Sea of Japan. This was a change. On Boxer, the task force had operated off the west coast of Korea, in the Yellow Sea. Now, operating in the Yellow Sea would place us too close to China for comfort.

The task force consisted of two aircraft carriers, USS Valley Forge and USS Philippine Sea, one heavy and two light cruisers, plus a dozen or more destroyers. The destroyers formed a ring of about three miles diameter around the carriers and cruisers, giving protection from both enemy submarines and aircraft. The entire task force followed the

Chapter 7   USS Valley Forge   121

movements of the carriers, all directed by the Admiral CTF 77, on the heavy cruiser.

My first combat mission on USS Valley Forge was flown on December 23, 1950. Of my many days in combat, which were to come, this would prove to be one of the worst.

First Mission Back

I was scheduled to fly as number four in LCDR Matthews' division. I would be flying right wing on the section leader, LTJG Charlie Melville. The other wingman, flying left wing on LCDR Matthews was scheduled to be Ensign Ray Svigel. Ray did not show up for the early briefing in the Ready Room. I told the XO I would go to the bunkroom and find Svigel. I went forward to the bunkroom looking for Svigel. I found him sound asleep in his bunk! I yelled and shook him, to no avail. He was in a top bunk at eye level. I grabbed his leg trying to pull him out of the rack. He coiled his leg, then struck out, hitting me in the chin, knocking me out. I woke up on the deck.

LCDR Matthews USS Valley Forge December 23, 1950

Chapter 7   USS Valley Forge

Now I was mad. I returned to the Ready Room and told the XO I could not wake Svigel. Ensign Bill Warwick was in the Ready Room, so he filled in for Svigel. This incident got Svigel a bad fitness report, which was not good for his career. But what he missed, was better missed.

Our intelligence briefing for this mission was emphatic, "Many Chinese troops reported at Chingyong on the outskirts of the port of Hungnam." Our Marines had been fighting their way out of this mass of Chinese. They were trying to get to safety aboard Navy transports, in Hungnam harbor. Our squadron crews had been working all night arming our Corsair fighters with napalm (jellied gasoline), fragmentation bombs and 50-caliber machine guns.

In the briefing, the XO stated that we would drop the napalm in division formation (four planes) on our first pass. We would then split up in sections (twos) to strafe with our 50-caliber machine guns.

The Korean Daddy with the Red Sweater

After launch, we rendezvoused over the ship and proceeded to the beach. It was a bright day with a high thin overcast. As we approached Hungnam, the XO contacted the forward air controller. We were directed to orbit.

Dutifully flying Melville's right wing, I was impatient to get into action. Shortly, we were sent north to our target, a road crossing west of Hungnam, with "many troops." We started a shallow dive toward the intersection. I set up my switches for napalm while hanging onto Melville's right wing. I glanced ahead to try to get a look at the target. As we approached the intersection, I could see we were very low (100 feet), so I stepped up on Melville's wing.

I could see a mass of "troops" ahead. I waited with my thumb on the bomb pickle. The XO transmitted, "Standby ... Mark," the signal to drop.

Four napalms exploded under us, turning the intersection into a ball of fire.

Chapter 7   USS Valley Forge

The XO pulled up left, Melville broke to the right. I was hanging tight to his right wing as he banked hard right, then left, dropping down low over a rice paddy, lining up perpendicular to the road. The road was raised six feet or more above the rice paddy. The road was packed with troops. I hung onto Melville's right wing, stepping up to avoid being dragged into the rice paddy, high enough to stay clear of his 50-caliber brass, which I knew would tumble out of his Corsair's wing as he fired. Melville opened up with his six machine guns, I did the same. The noise was terrific.

I was fighting to stay on Melville's wing while shooting at a couple hundred miles an hour. Our twelve machine guns had the effect of blowing the "troops" off of the road. They just disappeared.

Melville broke hard left, in a 70-degree bank staying low, I rode up on his right wing looking down through him at the ground as he pulled hard left tight and low, just above the telephone poles, banking steeply, setting up for another run. We were low over the road, in a 70-degree bank, just above the wires.

I saw a Korean man hanging on to the top of a telephone pole with his legs, WAVING A RED SWEATER over his head.

I had only the briefest glance, but the vision is still burned in my brain more than 60 years later. <u>He was warning me, they were not troops</u>! I pulled up and shouted on the radio, "Don't shoot, don't shoot. They are civilians." Some of the shooting stopped. But some did not.

We had been through this before on Boxer after Inchon. North Korean troops had changed into civilian clothes to escape our strafing. I made one more half-hearted pass on an ox cart, then circled above keeping an eye on the whole scene, repeating my warning.

We returned to the ship. I was sick at heart.

That night in the bunkroom, there were heated arguments on what had happened. Complicating the issue, during this

CHAPTER 7 **USS VALLEY FORGE**

mission, Ensign Bill Brinkley, of VF-63, one of my bunkroom buddies, had been shot down and killed, near our flight.

Ensign Buck Bustard of VF-63, one of Brinkley's close squadron friends, was so irate he broke chairs and other furniture in the bunkroom, refusing to believe they could be civilians. I argued that troops don't just stand in the road when being strafed and bombed, they go in the ditch. We never agreed on this, but he hadn't seen the; The Daddy with the Red Sweater.

History never recorded this tragedy. Our intelligence insisted they were troops, but many pilots disagreed. Today, no one will talk about it. There were thousands of Chinese troops in the area, but troops don't stand in roads with enemy aircraft in the vicinity. We know that thousands of North Koreans civilians, fleeing the Chinese, made it to the docks in Hungnam. Many of these survivors were transported to South Vietnam in Navy transports.

The Meredith Victory usually ferried such supplies as tanks, trucks, ammunition and troops during the Korean War. In December 1950 it carried 14,000 North Korean refugees to freedom.

I have included a picture from an article from the December 2002 issue of USAA Magazine, entitled "Voyage of Mercy." The article describes the SS Meredith Victory's rescue of thousands of North Korean refugees, who fled the Chinese

CHAPTER 7   USS VALLEY FORGE   125

army in December 1950. I believe these refugees were some of the survivors of our guns. What I witnessed were North Korean civilians, who knew the Communist Hell, who voted with their feet to even stand before our guns, rather than be Communist again.

I will carry the picture in my mind of, The Daddy with the Red Sweater forever. I saw him for just one instant. He is a real hero to me. Years later in Vietnam, he was a symbol to me, as I fought for another people who did not want to be Communist, the South Vietnamese. I also never, ever, automatically believed any intelligence briefing again. Thereafter, in Korea and Vietnam, I used my own eyes, made up my own mind and was very sure, before I pulled the trigger.

Lord, forgive me.

General MacArthur

January 1951 was unusually cold, stormy and snowy. The Marines fought their way south and were being evacuated out of Hungnam on Navy transports. They were taken south, off-loaded and redeployed north. Tens of thousands of North Korean civilians, who didn't want to be Communist, were also taken out on Navy transports. The Chinese troops continued their overwhelming assault south.

General MacArthur

To reverse the terrible situation, General MacArthur recommended bombing China with Air Force B29s and Navy squadrons to interdict the Chinese army's supply lines. He also recommended we unleash Chiang Kai-shek's trained troops in Taiwan eager to return to their home in mainland China.

These were reasonable recommendations. After all, the Chinese had attacked us in Korea without provocation.

President Truman refused.

MacArthur pushed the point hard, as he

Chiang Kia-shek

should have. On the eastern end of our lines, Army troops were cut off and suffered tens of thousands of casualties in the freezing weather, one of its worst defeats in U.S. history. The survivors reeled to the south. Seoul, fell to the Chinese.

My log book shows I flew only seven missions in January, most of these missions were close air support for Marines fighting in the cold and snow. The weight of the massed Chinese armies continued to push our troops south. President Truman and the press in general, blamed General MacArthur for the bad turn of events.

MacArthur's problems were very discouraging to those of us in the fight. However, our job was to support the troops in the field with close air support and interdiction of the roads, bridges and railroads. We did this to the best of our ability under difficult circumstances.

Shipboard Life

As fighter pilots, our lives on board revolved around the Ready Room, the flight deck, and the bunk room. It was a life I readily adapted to, and even thrived on. Fighter Squadron 24 was a tight knit group. The squadron training, briefing and debriefing were all done in the Ready Room. We stood watches at sea and ashore. The at sea watches, were Squadron Duty Officer, a twenty-four hour watch in the Ready Room and the Integrity watch, four hour watch on the flight deck. I was also assigned the duties of Assistant Flight Officer in the Operations Department.

As Assistant Flight Officer, I was responsible for making out the flight schedule for the next day's missions. Every evening at sea, after dinner, I would get a copy of the Air Plan from the Staff. The Air Plan assigned missions to each squadron for the following day. I would rough out the flight schedule, assigning pilots to each scheduled mission, showing the times of briefing, manning, takeoff and landing, the ordnance to be carried, etc. This task fit me perfectly. After dinner, most of the squadron stayed in the Wardroom, watching the movie. I have never cared for movies. When I completed the flight schedule, I would submit it to the Operations Officer, who reviewed it, then passed it to the Commanding Officer for signature. Now it was an Order. Each pilot was required to be on time and prepared for each briefing and mission.

This job gave me a unique insight into each pilot's individual capabilities and motivations. I could readily tell who was eager to fly and who was not just by the way they gave me grief if not flying, or the way they complained if they were assigned a tough mission. Mostly, there was great competition for missions among our squadron pilots. I enjoyed this job for the entire cruise. I made sure no one had more missions than me.

Teamwork

To many, from afar, it may appear that being a Naval Aviator, a fighter pilot, was glamorous. I quickly learned, as my fellow pilots did, we could die from shipboard operations or enemy fire, quickly and quietly, with little notice and no glamour. The war we were in had none of the glory of WWII (if there ever was), of an "Air War," where "Aces" (who shot others in the back) were elevated to ridiculous levels of heroism.

Air Group Two LSOs Zettle, Oliver and Tobin

Chapter 7   USS Valley Forge

We had little or no air opposition. However, on a daily basis we faced heavy enemy ground fire attacking targets such as bridges, trucks, trains or enemy troops. To stay alive, we depended not only on our own skills and those of our fellow aviators, but also on hundreds of shipmates to do their job to perfection. The squadron engine mechanics, airframe mechanics, ordnance men, plane captains, squadron operations, and administrative personnel were all vital to keeping us in one piece. The ship's catapult, arresting gear, fuel, and ordnance personnel all held our lives in their hands. I knew very few of these people personally. They never failed. Also, a strong faith was needed for sanity. I went to Mass daily. I also believed in the fight we were in. We fought for other people's freedom, people who did not want to be Communist. I slept well.

Catapult Launches (Cat Shots)

The preferred method of launching propeller aircraft was the deck launch. A loaded Corsair required about 550 feet of deck run with 25 knots of wind over the deck. At the beginning of each launch, the first fifteen or twenty aircraft had to be catapulted to gain the required space for deck launches.

Catapulting a VF-24 Corsair

On the last cruise, on Boxer, I had only been catapulted four times. It was a learning experience. Each "Cat Shot" terrified me. To catapult a Corsair safely required precise directions from the director taxiing the aircraft onto the catapult. The catapults at that time were giant slingshots, powered by large below-deck hydraulic rams run by an unseen crew. On deck, the catapult appears only as a slot in the deck that contains the "shuttle," which is attached to the hydraulic ram below. The shuttle has to be hooked to the aircraft by a wire rope "bridle." The director guides the pilot over the shuttle, where crewmen, working under the tail of the aircraft, attach a frangible "hold-back bar" to the aircraft's tail. The catapult officer signals "release brakes," a flicking of the right hand fingers. The pilot releases the brakes slowly, easing into the hold-back, so it won't fracture prematurely. The pilot depends solely on the hold-back bar to keep him from rolling into the ocean. It takes skill, and faith in the Cat crew. Simultaneously, other tough crewman brave the whirling 14-foot propeller, just feet away, fighting the blast of slipstream and wind over the deck to hook up the heavy wire rope "bridle" from the deck shuttle and to the Corsair's under-wing "Cat Hooks."

This must be done very quickly and precisely. The whole rig is "tensioned." The catapult officer gives the "tension" signal, a sweeping right hand down the deck, simultaneously flicking his left-hand fingers, meaning "brakes off." At this signal, the catapult crew captain eases the shuttle forward, tensioning the bridle against the Cat Hooks in the wings.

Once tensioned, the catapult officer waves two right-hand fingers overhead, asking for full power. Now, with my feet off the brakes, I go to full power, restrained only by the hold-back fitting, only green water visible over the nose. I salute and put my head back against the headrest...Wham... I'm flying.

My very life depended on those guys, most making less than $100 a month. They never failed.

Notes from my Aviator's Log Book January and February 1951

"Ensign Richter (VA-65) hit aft gun mount landing, sheared right wing"

"Close air support; strafed trawler, trucks, bombed powerhouse, napalmed storehouse"

"Spotted for Missouri"

"Spotted for Missouri" "Leveled Kowan north of Wonsan"

"Leveled Yongwol; bombs napalm"

Chapter 7   USS Valley Forge

"Vectored on B-29s no IFF"

"Spotted for Missouri. Spotted for DD Grapnel"

Ensign Sheehy (VF-24) hit pole while strafing, (he brought a piece of the pole back embedded in his wing)"

"Ensign Hofstra (VF-64) hit ground while strafing, ditched at sea, rescued after four hours by British flying boat"

"Ensign Martin (VF-24), catapulted with a 1000 pound bomb and eight wing bombs, pitched up, stalled, spun, lost at sea . (This ordnance load had been our standard for dive bombing bridges. It was determined that this load was too great for the Corsair and we shifted to 500 pound bombs)"

"LTJG McGoskie (VC-61), lost at sea, failed to return after a night attack mission"

"Ensign Stennett (VF-24) spun in at the 180 approaching the ship, he was rescued cold and wet"

"Ensign Tvede (VF-64) shot down Wonsan, rescued"

We were wearing rubber exposure suits on all flights. As the weather warmed, these suits were extremely hot and uncomfortable, to the point of heat prostration, in the non-air-conditioned Corsair. I routinely poured perspiration out of my exposure suit, after a three-hour flight. The suits had no ventilation, but they saved many pilots from the freezing water.

Gunfire Spot

Battleships, cruisers and even destroyers can shoot well beyond the visual range of the ship, therefore, they need aerial spotters to correct the fall of shot. The Corsair was an ideal aircraft for this mission. It was fast and tough enough to go into dangerous areas that had anti-aircraft guns or other defenses. It was also heavily

USS Missouri hammers Korean targets

Chapter 7   USS Valley Forge   131

armed and could stay on station for long periods of time.

Charlie Melville and I were the only two qualified naval gunfire spotters in the Air Group. On gunfire spot missions, I was usually scheduled as leader and given a wingman. This was great experience for me. Most of my contemporaries, Ensigns, were flying missions as wingman.

I spotted naval gunfire for the 16-inch guns of battleship USS Missouri on five occasions in February and March. Targets were near the coast, such as ship yards, bridges, train marshalling yards, factories and bridges. I would check in with the ship by radio, search for targets, then circle the target and call out a set of instructions called a "Fire Mission."

A Fire Mission consisted of the type of target, target coordinates, the number of guns required for adjustment, the type of ammunition, the fuse and the type of control. Normally, control was, "At my command will adjust." This meant the ship would read back the information, with the number of guns (usually two to adjust), type of ammunition and fuse, the time of flight, then state "Ready," when the guns were loaded and wait for me to call "Fire." I would time my orbit around the target to be at the far side from the falling shot. When the shots fell, I would estimate the miss distance, then call a correction (such as, "Right 200, Drop 100," in yards), then repeat firing, until the shots were on target. The call then was, "Fire for Effect." The ship would fire six to twelve rounds rapidly to destroy the target.

Naval gunfire is very accurate in deflection (left/right), but less accurate in range, because of its high velocity and flat trajectory. The fall of shot makes an oblong pattern, three or four times as long, as it is wide. Sixteen inch high-explosive projectiles weigh more than 2000 pounds. The effect of multiple 16-inch high explosive projectiles hitting the target, at supersonic speeds, was awesome. Although, the maximum range of a 16-inch gun was over 20 miles, this range was seldom used. Normal ranges were between 8 and 12 miles.

DD "Grapnel"

On March 20, 1951, I was scheduled for a memorable gunfire spot mission. The purpose of this mission was to

Chapter 7   USS Valley Forge   132

direct the 5-inch guns of a destroyer, "Call sign, Grapnel," in Wonsan Harbor. Wonsan is a large natural harbor on the east coast of North Korea, just north of the 39th parallel. Wonsan

Loaded VF-64 Corsair heads for Korean targets

Harbor had been surrounded by the Chinese as they pushed our forces south. Wonsan had many large and small islands within the harbor, some of which were still in our hands. The Navy maintained destroyers in and near Wonsan to provide fire support for these friendly islands. My wingman on this mission was our squadron Operations officer, LCDR Jim O'Brien. He had asked to observe a gunfire spot mission.

We launched, rendezvoused and proceeded to Wonsan. On checking in with "Grapnel" the ship informed me it had been fired on the previous evening by a battery of Chinese guns located on the south shore of the harbor. I reconnoitered in the area described, and found the Chinese guns hiding on the far side of a small hill. I set up a Fire Mission using two of Grapnel's 5-inch/38 caliber guns. We quickly bracketed the guns and I called "Fire for Effect." The gunfire did not totally destroy the gun battery because of its location in defilade (far side of the hill). Thereafter, I climbed to 8,000 feet with LCDR O'Brien on my wing. We each made several 45-degree dive-bombing runs dropping our 500-pound and 100-pound bombs on the gun battery. Between the 5-inch gunfire and our bombing, the gun battery was destroyed. We found several other targets for Grapnel's guns. We departed, satisfied with our mission. At the debriefing, LCDR O'Brien complemented me on the conduct of the mission.

On this mission, I had flown a Corsair from our sister squadron, VF-63. Flying a sister squadron's aircraft

Chapter 7   USS Valley Forge   133

happened infrequently, only when there were no Corsairs available from our own squadron. As I was leaving the Ready Room, the VF-63 Maintenance CPO came up to me and said, "Sir, your aircraft has some minor bomb blast fragments in the tail. Watch your low pull outs." I thanked the Chief for the information, and said I certainly would watch my pull outs. (A 500-pound bomb will blow fragments to 1,000 feet). In my exuberance to get good hits, I had gone too low.

Neither the CO, nor anyone else in VF-63, ever mentioned the minor bomb damage. However, I was surprised when, several days later, Lieutenant Bill Tobin, our flamboyant Air Group LSO, cornered me in the passageway and chewed me out about the bomb damage to the VF-63 aircraft. He was right. I held my tongue, he was a Lieutenant. That should have been the end of it. However, a few weeks later, LT Tobin flew one of our Corsairs on a Close Air Support mission. While making a napalm drop, on the deck, he set up his switches incorrectly and dropped six 100 pound bombs at an altitude of fifty feet, which nearly blew the bottom out of his Corsair. I never said a word to Lt Tobin.

Weather

The freezing cold and snow in March continued to limit our flying. Finding targets in the mountainous Korean landscape in the rotten weather was a challenge. Each rugged, snow-covered valley looked exactly the same. Frequently, we were forced to operate under low overcasts, where we were vulnerable to ground fire. Air Group aircraft were routinely hit by anti-aircraft guns and small arms. Our tough Corsairs and Skyraiders kept bringing us home.

Our luck held until the middle of March when Ensign Berglund VA-65 landed at Seoul airfield (Kimpo), badly shot up. Ensign Loomer (VF-24), was shot down and killed near the town of Kojo during a strike. Loomer had been my wingman on my first gunfire spot mission on September 16, 1950.

Finding our targets was difficult. We navigated only by dead reckoning (time, distance and heading) and map reading. There were no electronic aids. Our missions were scheduled for three hours, but frequently lasted longer. Carrier take-offs and landings were still taking as big a toll as the enemy. Ensigns Wallin and Knot VF-24 both had barricade crashes after missing the arresting wires.

Charlie Sato

Roughly once a month the ship would put into Yokosuka, Japan for R&R. The streets next to the harbor in Yokosuka in 1951 were bustling with every type of shop jammed one next to the other. We called this "Thieves' Alley." We all bought dolls, kimonos, jackets, lighters, and every kind of trinket for almost nothing. My favorite shop was a fishing gear store run by Charlie Sato and his wife. I frequented his shop so many times and bought so much fishing gear during our cruises on Boxer and Valley Forge that we became good friends. In later visits, when I would bring a Navy buddy into his store, he would take me aside and give me a small lure or a box of flies, and say, "Commissione," laugh and wink. Through the years, after many visits to Japan, I came to greatly admire and respect the Japanese people.

This picture of the sailor and the Japanese shopkeeper

Charlie Sato's Shop

A sailor in Thieves' Alley

reminds me of an incident that occurred during this period in Yokosuka. Ensign Buck Bustard and I were shopping in a similar shop when an obviously drunk American sailor came in and started to swear and berate the young female clerk. I ordered the sailor to stop his behavior. He put up a fight. Bustard went for the Shore Patrol as I tried to restrain the sailor. The sailor knocked me down and ran out of the shop with me in hot pursuit. We raced through the streets weaving through the crowds. Unfortunately for him, he ran around a corner right into the arms of the Shore Patrol and Bustard. They quickly subdued the sailor with their night sticks and off he went to the brig. Ah, American sailors at

CHAPTER 7   USS VALLEY FORGE   135

play.

USS Valley Forge Goes Home

At the end of March great news swept through the ship, "We are going home!" It was true, the USS Valley Forge was going home... but not with Air Group Two!

Air Group Two would transfer to USS Philippine Sea (CV-47), and remain in combat. Air Group Eleven, on USS Philippine Sea, would go home on USS Valley Forge.

We were disappointed, but we quickly got over it. Both USS Valley Forge and Air Group Eleven had been at sea longer than Air Group Two, so it was fair. The USS Valley Forge pulled into Yokosuka, Japan, under the hammerhead crane to make the initial transfer of squadron personnel and support equipment. (See the movie, "The Bridges at Toko Re," by Mitchner) This gave us a day or two liberty in Yokosuka, Japan.

The Plaque

Three weeks before our transfer to USS Philippine Sea, LCDR Matthews, our XO, directed me to the carpenter's shop, where the carpenters had prepared a very large, handsome piece of mahogany for a plaque. The XO gave me the task of designing and painting all the Air Group squadron insignias on the plaque. The plaque was to be presented to the Valley Forge, before Air Group Two departed the ship.

I needed help, fast. I enlisted a bunkroom friend Ensign John Kordeleski (of VF-64). Kordeleski was an excellent artist. Together, we commandeered one of the three bunkroom poker tables. Night after night, following our combat missions, Kordeleski and I painted the squadron and Air Group insignias on the large mahogany plaque. We took unending guff from our bunkroom buddies. We were taking their valuable card playing space.

The plaque was finished on time. It looked fantastic, due primarily to the great work of ENS John "Korday" Kordeleski. The Air Group put on a show in the Yokosuka Officer's Club when the plaque was presented. We acted mad. (We were!) The ship was going home without us. There were several raw skits. I recall Ensign Ed Hofstra reading a poem that ended, "Do not miss us, because you piss us, and we're glad to see you go." (Why do I remember that?) It was all in good fun and we were really very sorry to see USS Valley Forge go, it was a good ship. Valley Forge carried Air Group Two's plaque, proudly displayed on the hangar deck for almost another twenty years, until it was decommissioned in 1970.

ENS Leue' presents Air Group Two plaque to USS Valley Forge XO

In 1970, I was stationed in Virginia Beach serving as Commander Air Wing Seven. My neighbor and friend, Navy doctor, CDR McGreevy, bragged to me that he was going aboard USS Valley Forge, which was being decommissioned, to take off medical gear. He said, "I can get anything I want off that ship." I told him the story of the plaque and bet him he could not get it off. Two days later he presented me with the plaque. He had burned off the attachments with a welding torch! I carried the plaque with me for the next thirty-three years. I finally presented the plaque to the military museum at Santa Rosa Airport, California, during the Air Group Two Reunion in 2003. I dedicated the plaque as a memorial to Ensign John Kordeleski, who was shot down and killed attempting to rescue a downed Air Force pilot, during our final Korean combat cruise on USS Boxer in 1952.

Cross Deck Disaster

March 28, 1951. The Navy determined the easiest way to transfer the aircraft of the two Air Groups would be to go to sea, sail the Valley Forge and Philippine Sea on parallel

Chapter 7 USS Valley Forge

courses, five miles apart. Each ship would launch all aircraft, Air Group Two would fly to USS Philippine Sea then land, and Air Group Eleven would fly to USS Valley Forge and land. Simple, right? It turned into a disaster.

On the day of the transfer, there was almost no wind, but there was a very nasty steep swell from a Pacific storm. Air Group Eleven, on USS Philippine Sea, had F9F Panther jets, which required 30-plus knots of wind to launch and land. Both ships had to run at 30-plus knots into the swell. The result was the worst pitching deck I, or anyone else, had ever witnessed. The ships drove violently into the swells, taking white water over their bows, pitching and plunging wildly. These 800 foot plus, 45,000 ton ships, were pitching and tossing like little toy ships.

We deck launched, using 500-foot deck runs. LT Hugh Lowery launched in front of me. The Fly One, the Launching Officer, miss-timed Lowery's take off, he gave the launch signal as the bow was up, but then it quickly pitched down as Lowery roared down the deck. Lowery's Corsair disappeared into a tremendous wave, surging above the bow. Somehow, his Corsair plowed through the wave, shook off the sea, and staggered out the other side of the spray.

As I pulled up abeam the island, ready for my launch, I was wide eyed with anticipation. I said to myself, "You're not doing that to me!" When the Fly One gave me the signal to launch, the deck was down, I was looking down at green water! I put the stick in my lap and as soon as I felt lift, I snapped the gear up and tried to climb. This time, the Fly One had it right. The deck pitched up violently underneath me, my wheels were retracting and turning sideways, while dragging on the deck! My prop was only inches from the deck. The ship blew the crash horn. I flew away, oblivious. (Later, I was fully informed of my error by Skipper Coffman, who had been watching from Valley Forge's bridge.)

Landing on USS Philippine Sea was another challenge. Ensign Roland Robinson, of our squadron, who later would be my children's dentist, dove for the deck as it pitched up violently. He hit the deck so hard, he bent his Corsairs wings almost down to the deck. (He was a better dentist).

As I approached the USS Philippine Sea, the deck was pitching violently, our flight had to orbit as the crashed airplanes ahead of us were removed. Many attempting to land before me, took multiple wave offs. It was mayhem. I expected the worst.

However, as I made my first approach, the deck momentarily steadied, I took the cut from the LSO, and arrested.

Seconds later, as I taxied forward, the deck again started to pitch wildly. Water was cascading over the bow, washing down the deck. Taxiing forward and getting out of the cockpit was difficult. When I reached my spot, they directed to me to hold my brakes and stay in the cockpit.

Waves Wash Carrier's Warplanes
big wave breaks over the bow of the carrier Philippine ea, spraying planes on the big carrier's deck during operions off the Korean Coast. Planes had just returned from mbing mission against Reds. (AP Wirephoto)

This picture, of Philippine Sea in the Buffalo Evening News, was given to me in 2008, by my shipmate , Charlie Vullo. This day is March 28, 1951, the day of the cross deck, the only day USS Philippine Sea had these seas. The caption, "Returning from bombing Reds" was added by some journalist, for effect.

Chapter 7   USS Valley Forge

When my Corsair was tied down with chains, I jumped out, fighting my way toward the island, the pitching deck awash. I staggered, like a drunk, seawater sloshing through my legs, as planes waved off, landed and crashed. Once safely down below in the Ready Room, I was greeted by my squadron mates who were already aboard.

I found out that back on USS Valley Forge a landing F9F jumped the barricades, smashing into multiple aircraft up forward, setting fires and causing many injuries. Both Air Groups had crashes that damaged many airplanes on this day. Not a good operation.

Nevertheless, happy to be aboard in one piece, I found my way to the Junior Officer's Bunk Room, my new home, on the USS Philippine Sea.

Unknown to any of us, the worst fighting was yet to come.

Chapter Eight

USS Philippine Sea

Spring 1951

USS Philippine Sea, CVA-47, Sea of Japan, spring 1951

March 28, 1951. Air Group Two settled into USS Philippine Sea quickly. I was senior enough now to rate a six-man bunkroom, but I declined. I had become accustomed to the "casino-like" atmosphere of the forty-two man bunkroom, with several 45 rpm record players going simultaneously, a card game or two mixed with the discussions of politics or the day's combat missions. This was my home, and I felt comfortable. It was more difficult to feel sorry for myself in these surroundings. The ship's routine was the same as aboard the USS Valley Forge.

Massed Chinese troops had driven U.S. and U.N. troops well below the 38th parallel. Seoul, fell again to the Communists. This was war with China. The North Korean army had been defeated. General Walker, Commander Eighth Army under General MacArthur, was killed in a Jeep accident. He was replaced by General Ridgeway. Ridgeway, well-known for

CHAPTER 8   USS PHILIPPINE SEA   141

his aggressive style in World War II, brought a new optimism to the battle. Spring also brought a welcome improvement in the weather.

Ridgeway opened with a new offensive to drive the Chinese Communists north. However, on April 11, 1951, a week after our move to USS Philippine Sea, President Truman fired General MacArthur as Commander Far East and replaced him with General Ridgeway. General James Van Fleet took over Ridgeway's tactical command of the Eighth Army.

My pilot's log book for April 1951, shows 47.6 hours flown in combat. These missions were close air support for hard-

Korean bridges were bombed daily to stop the flow of supplies

fighting Marines, naval gunfire spotting for the battleship USS Missouri against coastal targets, armed reconnaissance, combat air patrol, and a major strike against the port city Hamhung.

Air Group Two and Fighter Squadron 24 were now a much more professional fighting team than when we started aboard USS Boxer at Inchon in September 1950. We had learned on the job in combat. The Air Group now looked good launching and recovering aircraft in minimum time, with minimum accidents and incidents. Our pilots were aggressive yet they had learned how to minimize losses by making simultaneous attacks on the main target and flak sites, limiting attacks to a single dive, by jinking (flying erratic courses and altitude) when under fire, by achieving

Chapter 8 USS Philippine Sea

F4U-4 Corsair struggles for altitude   Bill Crouse photo

tactical surprise by diving out of the sun, or from unexpected directions and minimizing low-altitude flying. Our maintenance crews had become professional and efficient in repairing, fueling, arming, servicing and launching our aircraft.

Our spirits were high. However, underlying this bravado was the sobering fact that we were in a war that our leaders had determined we would not win. General McArthur alone argued that the Chinese had attacked us and that we should respond by taking the fight to the Chinese mainland. The American people overwhelmingly supported McArthur. He returned home to a hero's welcome with massive ticker-tape parades. However, our objectives now could only be to hurt

VF-63 Corsair taxis forward after landing Spring 1951

CHAPTER 8   USS PHILIPPINE SEA

the Chinese, recover as much territory as possible and try to stay alive.

Our dilemma was obvious. We must fight aggressively and die if necessary, but there would be no grateful country, no Navy Cross as for those who died at Midway and Coral Sea in WWII. The realities of our situation not withstanding, my shipmates carried on their combat duties day in and out with high spirits and uncommon courage.

Loaded Skyraiders and Corsairs preparing for launch   B. Crouse photo

Under General Van Fleet's leadership, we drove the Chinese north through a combination of massive artillery, aggressive Army and Marine troops, devastating Air Force and Navy air support. In return, the Chinese stiffened their defenses by adding significantly to their anti-aircraft weapons. Our losses mounted.

Notes from my aviator's log book :

April 5th Ensign Tuthill (VF-64) hit over Wonsan, rescued, died of wounds.

April 11th Ensign (Woody) Brey, shot down central Korea, KIA.

April 17th Ensign Cosgriff shot down during large Air Group strike against Hamhung, rescued.

April 17th Ensign Dale Faler shot down Hamhung. KIA.

CHAPTER 8   USS PHILIPPINE SEA   144

Ensign Dale Faler

April 17, 1951. Ensign Dale Faler (VA-65) was shot down during the Hamhung strike. He was listed as killed in action. Several pilots saw his Skyraider hit, break up and go straight in. They swore he was dead.

They were wrong. After the cease-fire in 1953, Dale Faler was repatriated as a prisoner. He told me years later, in 1971 when we were both Captains serving in the Pentagon: "I was hit by AAA in my dive-bombing run. They blew the wing off my Skyraider. I was spinning and burning, the terrific G force pinned me in the cockpit. I said to myself, I don't want to die. With renewed strength I threw open the canopy, jumped, pulled the chute. It opened partially before I hit the river water. I went under immediately. When I came up the Chinese had guns trained on me. I was a prisoner."

He was lucky to live through his two years in prison. Only 35% of prisoners captured in Korea lived through their captivity. They were treated brutally. Kidding him years later, I said, "Thanks for the shaving cream." We would routinely pass out the toiletries of those bunkroom buddies shot down. He asked, "Who got my camera?" This surprised me. In all my time in the Navy I never had heard of anything taken. His camera should have been packed and sent with his personal effects to his next of kin.

Skipper, LCDR Emery R. Coffman

LCDR Emery Coffman, CO VF-24

LCDR Emery Coffman, Fighter Squadron 24's Commanding Officer, was a giant to us. He was a big man, physically and professionally. We knew he had played football for Alabama in the Rose Bowl, had fought in World War

CHAPTER 8   USS PHILIPPINE SEA   145

II in the Pacific, and had gallantly led us for two years beginning at Oceana, Virginia. His good judgment and high spirits carried us through our first combat on USS Boxer, our rapid emergency deployment and hard fighting on USS Valley Forge, our unexpected transfer to USS Philippine Sea and the loss of our shipmates along the way. He was a great Skipper.

April 20, 1951. During a routine armed reconnaissance mission near Wonsan Harbor, LCRD Coffman's Corsair was hit in the wing by 37 mm cannon fire. The hit severely damaged his left aileron. He managed to fly over Wonsan Harbor, where he attempted to bail out. Ensign Bill Hugo, his wingman, told me later the Skipper cautioned him not to join too close because he was having trouble controlling his damaged Corsair. When the Skipper released the control stick to jettison his canopy (it took two hands), his Corsair snapped violently into a spin. He was pinned in the cockpit by high gee forces. He spun with the airplane into Wonsan Harbor and was killed. His body was recovered by a U.S. destroyer while under Communist fire in Wonsan Harbor. He was buried at sea.

This was a severe blow to the squadron. Skipper Coffman was a calm, modest, strong, and steady leader. He was my model of a combat leader. LCDR Matthews, our Executive Officer, took over our squadron, VF-24. This was a difficult position for LCDR Matthews. He was taking over the squadron in combat from a very popular and respected leader. I observed LCDR Matthews closely during this trying period, what he said to the squadron and how he handled himself. It was on-the-job training for me. Years later, in a place called VietNam, I would be faced with the same challenge.

Flak for Breakfast, Lunch and Dinner

Another bunkroom friend, Ensign West (VF-63), was shot down in central Korea April 24, during a close air-support mission. He was reported "Missing in Action." Later this was changed to "Killed in Action." The bunkroom was not as crowded as it once was.

All of our losses were from heavy, concentrated anti-aircraft fire from rapid-fire weapons of 50-caliber to 85-mm. The rapid-fire 37mm was the most prevalent and deadly weapon. It appeared to pilots as streams of red or orange balls of fire. The 37-mm could shoot effectively up to 4,000 feet altitude. The 85-mm was a bursting flak that looked like dirty black clouds. It could shoot to 25,000 feet. We called all anti-aircraft "flak." All these weapons were made in Russia or China. Most were visually sited, but the larger calibers could

Smoke rises from a strike on Chinese positions, LTJG Jimmy Dick

be radar directed. The gunners were very good; they had all kinds of practice. To bomb and strafe, as we all did on our missions, required that we dive through fields of fire of these weapons, thus we were vulnerable in each and every dive, on every mission.

Enemy aircraft were never a significant threat. The Russian Mig flying from North Korean airfields was too short legged (lacked range) to come down to engage us. The few that did, were never a threat to us. We could take care of ourselves. (A Marine Corsair pilot shot down a Mig who made the

Chapter 8 USS Philippine Sea

mistake of attacking him.) We considered the highly publicized Mig/F86 hassles over the Yalu a sideshow. To us, the thousands of missions being flown from Navy Carrier decks each month in support of the Marines and Army troops on the front lines was the real air war.

General Van Fleet's strategy was showing results. U.S. Marine, Army, Republic of Korea and United Nations troops, with heavy air support had stopped the Chinese and were now driving them north. May 1951 featured massive close air support with napalm to support Marines struggling in the mud below. This inflicted terrible losses on the Chinese. Increased Chinese anti-aircraft fire returned the favor.

Ensign Lowell Elmore

Logbook- May 18, 1951, five aircraft shot down this day.

Ensign Lowell Elmore

One of them was Ensign Lowell Elmore of VF-24.

Ensign Elmore was VF-24's "Bull" or senior Ensign. He was an excellent combat leader of his own division of four Corsairs. On this particular day, his division was directed to attack several U.S. half-track anti-aircraft vehicles that had been captured by the Chinese when they broke through the Republic of Korea lines the previous night.

Elmore's division was diving on these half-tracks firing their 50-caliber machine guns. The half-tracks returned the fire. Elmore's gas tank, 235 gallons of 115/145 octane, just in front of him, blew up. He pulled up, threw off his canopy and bailed out. Ensign Brown, his wingman, told me later Elmore almost went though Brown's prop when he bailed out, Brown was so tight on Elmore's right wing.

CHAPTER 8   USS PHILIPPINE SEA   148

Elmore's section leader, LTJG Stan Bueg, called the rescue net for a helicopter. Stan Bueg, Brown and the rest of the division strafed to keep the Chinese away from Elmore. Elmore was picked up by a rescue helicopter but this helicopter was also hit by the Chinese fire and damaged. The rescue helo went down again on the way back to our lines. Ensign Brown and LTJG Bueg, low on gas, had to depart, not knowing whether Elmore made it back alive or not.

Days went by with no word on Elmore.

GIs FOOD

Six days later, on May 24, I was scheduled for a gunfire-spot mission with the battleship USS Missouri in the same area Elmore had been shot down. Skipper Matthews asked me to take some time at the end of my mission to look for Elmore. Ensign Svigel was my wingman on this mission. We launched, rendezvoused over the ship and headed for the position of the USS Missouri off the east coast of Korea.

I found the Missouri, checked in by radio and was informed their helicopter was missing over the beach. We were asked to look for it. I replied, "Affirmative." However, this didn't make Svigel and me happy. We were looking forward to doing some damage to the Chinese, then looking for Ensign Elmore. We searched for the Missouri's helicopter for about an hour with no luck. Then the Missouri advised they had found their helo. It was not lost it just had a radio problem. This released Svigel and me to look for Elmore.

We headed for the area where Elmore had disappeared, the nearby town of Ingy, about five miles inland from the east coast of Korea, just above the 38th parallel. I put Svigel about a quarter mile off my right wing. Shortly, Svigel spotted a flashing light off to my left. It appeared to be a signal mirror or gun muzzle flashes.

I told him to go high and cover me, I would get a closer look.

The Chinese were known to set up flak traps, where they would set out a juicy target with many concealed guns all around, so I was cautious. Going lower, I saw what looked like a sign on the side of a hill. I made a still lower pass. There appeared to be white sheets, spelling, "GI Food." I made a another low, fast pass. There were troops in trenches below the sign.

This was in the area where the half-tracks were captured, and Elmore was shot down. I had to determine whether this was Elmore or maybe other GIs or even Chinese. After several high-speed passes, I decided it was safe enough to go slower. I put down part flaps opened my canopy then flew past the troops very close, low and slow, about 100 feet and 120 knots. They could have easily shot me down. I looked them in the eye. They were waving at me, they were GIs!

I called Svigel and directed him to climb, call the rescue net and ask for helicopters. Svigel called repeatedly, but the rescue net simply said, "Wait." After an extended delay, the rescue net informed us no helos were available. They gave no explanation. Later, I learned they did not believe we could tell they were our troops.

In frustration, I climbed high enough to contact the ship and requested permission to land for food or help at a nearby emergency strip, Kangnung, (K18). This request was granted. Svigel and I flew to K18. We landed on the short, narrow, perforated, steel runway (Marsten Matt). We had not landed on a runway ashore in five months, and it showed. I made my first pass with my hook down out of habit. Svigel hit a runway light and blew a tire. I taxied up beneath the little temporary tower the Marines had placed by the runway. I jumped out and was immediately confronted by a gruff Marine Sergeant.

He began to laugh and said, "I can't believe they let school kids fly those things!" I was not pleased. Maybe we looked young, but at that point we had survived years of tough fighting. I held my temper and explained what we had found on the side of the nearby hill. The Sergeant immediately said he knew who the troops in the trenches were. He said they were his buddies, advisors to the Republic of Korea troops in

Chapter 8 USS Philippine Sea

that sector. He figured the ROK troops had fled and left his buddies high and dry. He assembled a crew and devised a scheme to tie cases of C rations on our bomb racks with parachute cord. We took off and flew very slowly with our gear down and dropped the C rations on the hill. The troops were gone! We made a high-speed pass, did a roll as a salute and departed for our landing or "Charlie Time" on Phil Sea.

VF-24 Pilots, USS Philippine Sea, CO LCDR Matthews.

I had a guilty feeling going back to a clean warm bunk while those guys were still lost behind enemy lines. I never knew what happened to them.

Ensign Elmore Found

We debriefed with the Air Intelligence Officer and told Skipper Matthews our story. We did not find Elmore. About a week later, we received a message that informed the squadron Elmore was in the hospital ship in Yokosuka or Pusan.

Later, in port at Yokosuka, Japan, when we welcomed Elmore back aboard, he told us the rest of the story. He had been picked up by a second helo after his first rescue helo was damaged by enemy fire. He had lost his dog tags and most

CHAPTER 8   USS PHILIPPINE SEA   151

of his fight suit in his high-speed bailout. He was also burned. The medics saw how young he was, a mess, burned, with no uniform. They concluded he was an enlisted Marine running from his outfit. They didn't believe he was a Naval Officer. They put him in an enlisted ward. This made Ensign Elmore very angry, but he had no dog tags or other ID, so that's where he stayed. He was happy to be back, and we were very happy to have him back.

Rumors

As May progressed, the rumors that we may go home increased. No one would say how long we might stay in combat. Everyone was afraid to guess. It was the topic of most wardroom and bunkroom discussions. The Air Group had started on USS Boxer in the summer of 1950, then returned on USS Valley Forge, then transferred to USS Philippine Sea in April 1951. Skipper Coffman, who had first briefed us in Oceana, Virginia, when the war started, that we would not go to Korea, was dead, as were many others. Still we continued the offensive against the Chinese with predominately close air support missions. We lost LTJG Ball (killed) and LT Osborne (captured) in the middle of May. Despite the uncertainty and the losses, we were in relatively good spirits. We knew we were being effective against the Chinese. Our lines moved forward at a steady rate.

Combat Air Patrol, A Night Landing

Combat Air Patrol (CAP), or flying air defense for the task force, was not my favorite mission. This was generally a boring flight orbiting under radar control, only occasionally being vectored to check out suspicious targets.

However, on one CAP mission late in the afternoon, things got interesting. LT Bruce Robertson was the fight leader. I was flying number three or section leader. Late in the mission, we were vectored to the beach. An Air Force B-26 had been shot down west of Wonsan and they needed us for Rescue Combat Air Patrol (Rescap). As we headed for the beach the sun was setting. LT Robertson's radio failed so he passed me the lead. We were switched to the Air Force fight's frequency. The B-26 leader gave me directions to the area of the downed B-26. He explained that his wingman had been hit, the crew had bailed out and were holed up in the rugged area ten miles west of Wonsan. He had seen the chutes, but did not then have the crew in sight, nor have any communications with them. He was certain they were alive and had requested a helicopter from the "Barge," an LST in Wonsan Harbor, where the Navy always kept a rescue helo ready. (See "The Bridges at To-Ko-Re" by Mitchner).

Although it was getting dark, I found the B-26 leader orbiting the site of the bail out. He was low on fuel and had to depart for his base, but requested we continue to search for his wingman's crew and stand by to protect the rescue helo when it arrived. Shortly, the rescue helo checked in, reporting his position several miles to the east of the crash site. Our flight of four Corsairs searched as best we could in the fading light. We still had no contact with the B-26 crew on the ground. I reported this fact to the helo. I could hear the fear in the helo pilot's voice as he proceeded over hostile territory in the fading light. He was extremely vulnerable in an area in which a well-armed B-26 had been shot down.

We escorted the helo over the shoot-down site. The helo pilot searched for five minutes at low level but reported, "No Joy." We escorted the helo safely back to Wonsan then

ENS Dave Leue' taxis forward after landing

Chapter 8   USS Philippine Sea   153

departed for the ship. Now I had to think about my own flight. It was now very dark.

Naval fighter squadrons did not fly at night during this era of straight carrier decks. It was too dangerous landing a standard day fighter on a straight carrier at night. Each ship had a four-plane night fighter detachment with specially equipped aircraft, radars and autopilots. Also, night pilots had special training. We had neither the special aircraft nor the training.

I tuned in the YG/ZB homer, checked the sector for the correct code, then led the flight back to the ship. This would be the first night carrier landing for all of us. I spotted the USS Philippine Sea's truck lights (masthead) at about three miles, the Captain had kept the ship in the wind waiting for us. The night procedures mimicked day procedures, which I knew well. There was no radar control.

I asked for the ship's heading and turned the flight to come up the ship's wake letting down to 500 feet on the radio altimeter. I put the flight in right echelon, then broke left ahead of the bow. I let down to 150 feet on the down wind, turning base as the ship's truck lights passed abeam, using the radio altimeter I let down to 75 feet at the 90-degree position picking up the lighted paddles of LT Zettle, our excellent LSO. Zettle picked me up with a "high" signal, I eased it down to a "Roger," picking up the dustpan deck lights in close. Cut! I was aboard. Amazingly, the entire flight got aboard the first pass.

LT Zettle complemented us at the debrief in the Ready Room. There was a feeling of deep satisfaction marred by memories and vague feelings of guilt. The B-26 crew were dead or captured, somewhere in the dark, in the cold hills of North Korea, while I was heading for the Wardroom and a warm meal.

LTJG Charlie Melville

I've lost track of exactly when this mission took place, but it stands out for two reasons: first, LTJG Charlie Melville did an

CHAPTER 8   USS PHILIPPINE SEA   154

LTJG Charlie Melville 1951

outstanding job of gunfire spotting for the battleship USS Iowa; second, I got us in trouble with the Admiral, on USS Iowa. The mission was also unusual for being very far north of our normal operating area.

I was excited about the mission. It was against three bridges, two railway and one highway bridge, only twenty miles south of the Manchurian border. The battleship USS Iowa would be the firing ship. We may see Migs way up there.

We launched and proceeded north of Chongjin to Churinjang at the extreme northeastern tip of Korea. I did not see a Mig, but what I did see turned out to be better.

Charlie was senior, so he directed the "Fire Mission" with the USS Iowa. He proceeded to expertly direct the Iowa's 16-inch guns, knocking down all three bridges in less than an hour. Meanwhile, I was free to attack the town of Churinjang.

I found factories in full operation. Obviously they were not expecting us and were so far north the town had never been hit before. There was a steel mill, many railroad cars, a steam locomotive and many other targets. There was no anti-aircraft fire.

I was armed with our standard load of one 500-pound bomb and eight 100-pound wing bombs and my six 50-caliber machine guns.

I first bombed the steel mill, then strafed and blew up the locomotive and generally raised "Cain," strafing and bombing the rail yard with multiple runs. All this should have gone unnoticed. However, in my youthful exuberance, I decided to

Chapter 8   USS Philippine Sea   155

USS Iowa bombards Korean targets

describe my attacks to the sailors listening on the USS Iowa gunfire-spot frequency, who I imagined never saw or heard the war first hand. I described my bombing and burning the steel mill. I went so far as to key my mike, so they could hear the wild din as I fired all six 50-caliber machine guns strafing the locomotive. I then described the scene as the locomotive blew up!

We were taught strict radio discipline. This was a flagrant violation. At the time, it seemed like a good idea. We were way up north a long way from the fleet. I did not realize there was an Admiral listening on board USS Iowa. My performance did not please the Admiral. Charlie should have received some sort of award, a Distinguished Flying Cross (DFC), at least, for downing three bridges on a single mission. Thanks to his wingman, what he got was a nasty message from Commander Bombardment Force, USS Iowa to CTF 77, relayed by message, which was relayed to our Ready Room teletype:

From: CTF Bombardment Group

To: CTF-77

"UNUSUALLY POOR RADIO DISCIPLINE EXHIBITED BY ALAMEDA SPOT SIX DURING IOWA SHOOT TODAY"

CHAPTER 8   USS PHILIPPINE SEA

Close Air Support for Marines

May 23, 1951. The Marines were locked in bitter battles for the hills just south of the 38th parallel near the Hawachon reservoir in central Korea. On this mission, I flew right wing on LCDR Bill Matthews, our Commanding Officer. I am not certain of the section leader and other wingman. Probably they were LT Bruce Robertson and ENS Bill Warwick. We were each armed with one napalm tank, eight fragmentation bombs and 2,400 rounds of 50-caliber ammunition, a typical close-air support load. We were briefed to rendezvous over the ship then proceed to a point in central Korea, orbit and wait for calls from Marine forward air controllers. These forward controllers were all Marine Naval Aviators in the trenches with radios, trained to direct Navy and Marine fighter aircraft against enemy troops. This was a very effective tactic, especially when the Marines were facing overwhelming odds, as they were against the massed Chinese attacks.

On this mission, we proceeded south of the front lines near the Hawachon Reservoir in central Korea, as briefed, and orbited at 5,000 feet on station waiting for a call.

We were quickly called by a Marine unit, Call Sign "Seeder Bird 14." The "14" indicated this was a ground controller.

A division of Corsairs heads for close air support mission

Seeder Bird 14 requested quick assistance. His platoon was pinned down on a ridge running north-south, under heavy mortar and machine gun fire. I could hear the rattle of machine guns and the boom of mortars when he keyed his mic to talk. He said he was lying on his back looking up, trying to spot us. He described his position as on a north-

Chapter 8   USS Philippine Sea

south ridge with the Chinese at the north end of the tee. He advised the Marines had placed highly colored panels by their foxholes. The visibility was terrible, smoky and murky from the fighting.

Seeder Bird 14 said he could not raise his head from his foxhole to look for us because of the fire. LCDR Matthews, who didn't have the best eyesight, said he could not find the Marine position and passed the lead to me when I volunteered that I thought I knew their location. Seeder Bird 14 said, "Navy 418, I can hear your engines, turn south!" He directed me to turn this way then that. I followed his directions. Then, off to my left, I saw the Marines high visibility panels on the tee ridge. Seeder Bird 14 said, "Navy 418, I can see you. Make dummy runs, no ordnance drops, until I'm sure you are dropping on the Chinese, not us". I "Rogered," then led the flight on several dummy runs "on the deck," keeping the panels just off my left wing.

Seeder Bird 14 liked the dummy runs and requested a single napalm drop on my next pass. He wanted me to put my napalm right in the "crotch" of the tee, 50 yards in front of the Marines. I made my run. The napalm blew up right in the crotch, then spilled burning napalm down the slope on the Chinese.

Seeder Bird 14 was ecstatic. I put the flight into a tail chase, passing the lead back to LCDR Matthews. Seeder Bird 14 directed each following aircraft to drop slightly right or left on the tee ridge. He then directed us to drop our fragmentation bombs on the down slope parallel to the top of the tee. Then he requested strafing. We strafed repeatedly with our 50-caliber machine guns. We made dozens of runs, finally running out of ammunition. I reported this fact to Seeder Bird 14. He said, "Keep making runs, they are still running!" I now made my runs with the Marines to my left, parallel to the top of the tee, diving and pulling out below the ridge, showing off.

Looking up, I saw the Marines, who, minutes before could not look over the edge of their foxholes, standing up as in grandstands, watching the show, waving, cheering us on. No troops could stand up to the Navy-Marine team.

I felt great and I imagine the Marines felt much better. Low on fuel, we departed, Seeder Bird 14 thanked us profusely.

Unfortunately, upon return from this mission we found that not a mile from us, two of our shipmates, LTjg Jimmy Dick and ENS Murphy, of VF-64, flying similar close-air support, collided and were killed in the smoke and haze as they flew in support of another group of embattled Marines.

Going Home

We had no way of knowing then, nor could anyone know, the fighting just south of the Hawachon Reservoir, would continue in a see-saw stalemate with the Chinese, over this same ground, for two more years. Tens of thousands of lives would be lost. A decision had been made at the highest level *not* to pursue the Chinese past the 38th parallel.

General McArthur, who said, "There is no substitute for victory," had come home a hero to the American people. President Truman's ratings dropped to less than 30%.

Toward the end of May 1951, we received word that, at last, we would be returning to the USA. The ship stopped briefly in Yokosuka, Japan, where I called Jane to tell her the good news. We made hurried plans to be married toward the end of June.

I went ashore one last time to buy pearls and china for Jane and presents for family and friends. Of course, I also stopped to see my friend, Charlie Sato, in his fishing shop in "Thieves' Alley" to buy more of his fishing gear. I bought two fly rods from him, the best and the cheapest split bamboo fly rods he

Thieves alley Yokosuka Japan

Chapter 8 USS Philippine Sea

offered. I still have the former, retired, after years of faithful fishing, "Emeritus."

I knew deep down Air Group Two and I would be back in combat with the Chinese in Korea within the year. I forced that knowledge into the back of my mind. I wanted to see only good things ahead.

The USS Philippine Sea followed the shortest route, the Great Circle, and broke speed records crossing the Pacific to home!

CHAPTER NINE

Marriage, Panther Jets

The USS Philippine Sea broke records getting us home, averaging more than 25 knots for the entire trip. Still, it seemed an eternity. We entered San Francisco Bay June 10, 1951.

USS Philippine Sea passes under the Bay Bridge June 10, 1951

Earlier, betting that I would survive the cruise, I had purchased a brand-new, tailor-made gabardine uniform in Yokosuka to wear for this event. If I didn't survive, it wouldn't make any difference. I had hung the uniform up in one of the lockers in the JO bunkroom. I shared this locker with about ten others. Just before muster on our day of arrival in San Francisco, with great anticipation, I went to the locker to don my new uniform. I found, to my dismay, the uniform had been worn, was dirty, wrinkled, and the pants were torn at the pockets. One of my bunkroom buddies, in need of a clean uniform for liberty in Yokosuka, had worn it. Whoever it was, obviously heavier than I, had a very good time. I put on my old uniform for entering port. Later, I had

Chapter 9   Marriage, Panther Jets   161

my "new" uniform cleaned and pressed, then I personally sewed up the split seams. I was disappointed, but I thanked the Good Lord that I was there to wear anything.

San Francisco gave the USS Philippine Sea and Air Group Two a big welcome as it passed under the Golden Gate Bridge and tied up at Alameda Naval Air Station. I don't recall how I travelled home to Buffalo. I probably hopped a Navy flight out of Alameda.

Buffalo, Marriage Preparation

Coming home was a particularly joyous event. Jane and I had been engaged for almost four years. We both had a hard time believing we would finally be married. We had been separated much of the four years, with the final year filled with the uncertainty of battle.

I asked Joe Zawotoski, my Catholic college buddy, to be my best man. My college roommates, Jim Carr and Vince Larusso, Jane's uncle, Bill Littlefair, and my brother-in-law, Speas Anderson, agreed to be groomsmen. Gordon Sales had moved away from Buffalo and was not able to attend.

Jane and her stepmother, Vera, had been working on the arrangements for weeks. The marriage Mass was to be held at Saint Benedict's Catholic Church in Buffalo, Jane's parish. The reception would be held at the Brookfield Country Club, where Arnold and Vera Febrey were members. Jane's dress, the flowers, invitations and other details were in various stages of completion.

Joe agreed to be my best man, on one condition. I had to agree to the Polish tradition, the best man and the groom must sleep in the same room the night before the wedding. He explained that this ensured that no one would steal the groom! I laughed. Who would steal me? I went along with his wishes. Since I last saw him, I had a small taste of what he had suffered in combat, so my respect for him had grown immensely. I apologized for our fight over his prediction that "I would fight the Communist." How right he was!

CHAPTER 9 MARRIAGE, PANTHER JETS

Jane and I went shopping for a car. Jane's father helped us find an almost new, black 1950 Ford coupe, at reasonable price. Jane and I had a maintained joint account for four years, so we had enough cash for the car, to help with the wedding expenses and have enough left over for the honeymoon. It was an "all-cash" world. There were no credit cards and no one outside of your hometown would take a check.

Wedding

Wedding Mass   David and Jane   ghostly Father Tobin

Arnold Febrey, Jane Febrey   Ensign & Mrs. Leue'

The wedding Mass took place the morning of June 30, 1951. It was a beautiful ceremony. Father Tobin said the Mass. The reception followed at the Brookfield Country Club. The wedding and reception were simple, but beautiful. Jane and I both had a hard time believing this was really happening.

Dave and Jane leave the reception

Reception

The reception at Brookfield Country Club was elegant, modest, with hors d'oeuvres and drinks for family and close friends. Guests included: Mr. and Mrs. Alf (my former landlords, who had asked Joe, Jim, Vince Gordon and I to leave their upper flat for making too much noise); Mr. and Mrs. Bill Graham (my aunt and husband); Mr. and Mrs. Bill Groom (Jane's birth mother's family; Mr. and Mrs. Glen Gannon (Jane's aunt and uncle), for total of about forty-five. Jane and I stayed a respectful period of time with our family and friends, thanked all present, then made our departure.

The night before the wedding, we had packed our car with all of our clothes and wedding gifts, then hid it where no one

Chapter 9 Marriage, Panther Jets

could find it. Our plans were to spend our first night at the Hilton in downtown Buffalo. We arrived at the Hilton and I had our car parked by the valet. Checking in, I was surprised the head Bell Hop at the Hilton was a buddy from my old neighborhood on Virgil Avenue. I hadn't seen him since high school. I thought the jig was up. We would be harassed. Instead, my old friend had a grand bouquet of flowers sent up to us.

Cross-Country Honeymoon

The next day, we departed Buffalo and followed the lake shore route through Erie Pennsylvania, Sandusky and Cleveland, Ohio, then to Chicago, Illinois. This took us three days. We visited with my Uncle Ally, Aunt Loretta and Cousin Carol Hanser in Winnetka, just north of Chicago. They had moved into a beautiful new home on the edge of town. They gave us a beautiful set of the very best kitchen cookware for a wedding present. I had left their household in Winnetka just nine years earlier, as a youngster. This was a happy reunion. My aunt and Carol were very anxious for us to stay and visit for several days. Loretta suggested we visit my old friends Don and Bobby Harnsberger, but I demurred.

I should have agreed and stayed, but I said we had to be on our way. Ally and Loretta had always treated me like a son. I never properly acknowledged their great kindness. However, for what-ever reason, I said we had to move on after a day.

Tourists watch bears, Yellowstone Park

We followed the northern route through Yellowstone Park, where we stayed two days. We hiked, fished, cooked trout over a fire in our own skillet, saw Old Faithful, took

CHAPTER 9   MARRIAGE, PANTHER JETS   165

pictures of bears and generally enjoyed the beauty of the lakes and mountains.

This was a special time. We had waited and now were enjoying life as two young lovers. Jane was twenty-one and this was the first time she had been out of the near-confines of her family in Buffalo. This was a big adventure for her in more ways than one. The trip to Santa Rosa, California, took two weeks. We shared the driving. We had one small mishap in the rain in a small Midwestern town. Coming down a hill, Jane slid into a car stopping at stop light. There were no seat belts so we ended up on the dash, with our wedding presents and luggage pressing the seat backs against us. We got out and looked but there was only minor damage. Cars in those days had real bumpers that minimized damage from that sort of contact. We apologized. The people in the car we bumped saw we were newlyweds, smiled and said, "Don't worry about it."

The trip was wonderful. Everything we owned in the world was in our car, with the exception of my uniforms in the BOQ in Santa Rosa.

When we arrived in Santa Rosa, we immediately began looking for an apartment. We had arrived in town several days after Rube Brogan and Bill Warwick and their brides. It seemed as though everyone in the Air Group had gone home and been married ahead of us. Most of the available housing was taken. Jane and I stayed a night or two in a motel looking for a place to rent. Sally and Bill Warwick found a nice one-bedroom apartment over a garage. We looked at another apartment, but Rube and Joan Brogan had taken it. Fortunately, a day later, Bill and Sally Warwick found a house they liked better, so Jane and I happily moved into the one-bedroom garage apartment they had vacated.

Naval Auxiliary Air Station Santa Rosa

The squadron was stationed at the Naval Auxiliary Air Station, Santa Rosa. It had been a World War II Naval Air Station, and had been re-activated for the Korean War. Santa Rosa, surrounded by gently rolling oak-covered hills,

CHAPTER 9 MARRIAGE, PANTHER JETS 166

forty miles north of San Francisco, was a small, beautiful, sleepy town. It was an ideal area for young lovers, with wonderful weather, hidden valleys, wineries, close by beaches and the Russian River. There was only one dark cloud on the horizon. The Korean War was still raging. Our Air Group would be returning to combat in six months, aboard USS Boxer.

Jane and Dave 1951

We put the "dark clouds" out of our minds and quickly settled into the routine of a married couple. Jane arranged things in our new home and got to know the other wives in the squadron.

We continued flying our Corsairs daily, keeping up our skills, while studying the Grumman F9F-2 Panther jet that we were scheduled to fly. None of the squadron pilots had flown a jet. Two new pilots with jet experience, LCDR Ray Volpi and LT Morrison, a full-blooded Cherokee Indian, joined the squadron to help in our transition training. A new commanding officer, LCDR Ray Conklin, took over VF-24 from LCDR Matthews, who had served as CO after LCDR Coffman's death.

Carrier Air Group Two was the only Air Group stationed at Santa Rosa. The flying rules were very lax. We had been in combat for more than a year and were feeling our oats. I recall returning to base in a Corsair and asking for a low pass, which was granted. As I was buzzing the runway at 200 feet, I looked up and saw another Corsair buzzing the runway at 200 feet coming the other way. We each broke right and went on our way. Nobody said a word.

Floppy

Shortly after we arrived in Santa Rosa, California, Jane and I, like many newly married couples, wanted a pet. We bought a beautiful liver-and- white Springer spaniel. We named him Floppy. Floppy was a sweet dog, very well behaved and he

Chapter 9   Marriage, Panther Jets

Jane & Floppy

fit easily into our little garage apartment. I had visions of making Floppy a hunting dog. Having no knowledge of training dogs, this effort was a miserable failure. One Sunday, after Mass, Jane and I took Floppy and a shotgun to a deserted section of the beach west of Santa Rosa, near Jenner. I shot off my 20 gauge. Floppy took off and never stopped until he hid under our car about a mile away. Nevertheless, Floppy was a loyal companion and he turned out to be especially so for Jane when I deployed back to Korea several months later.

Santa Rosa, New Friends

Santa Rosa, California, is beautiful at any time a year, but for two recently married youngsters, July, August and September were glorious. On weekends, Jane and I would travel the short distance to the coast to the Russian River and Jenner. We would spend the day touring the backcountry in our 1950 two-door Ford or walking the beach or swimming, stopping for a hamburger or soft drink, just enjoying the beautiful countryside, the weather and each other. It was a magical time and it was even sweeter because we knew within a few months I'd be off to war again.

Jane relaxing at Jenner beach 1951

Chapter 9 Marriage, Panther Jets 168

Air Group Two Party, Herman and Helen Radtke left & right

We socialized with other young married couples in our squadron and air wing. Jane got to know most of the young wives in VF-24 including Joan Brogan, Sally Warwick, Helen Radtke, Maria Volpi and Mona Dudek. These young ladies would become a mutual support group when we deployed to Korea in a few months. Sometimes we got together at each other's homes, at other times at the officers club at the base. The ladies were drawn together by the same camaraderie that my squadron buddies and I felt. We had an important mission and shared a common cause with difficult challenges, separation and danger. It drew us together and we became lifelong friends.

New Home, Almost

During this period of time we found a brand-new house that was almost finished in Santa Rosa proper. The three-bedroom home, being built by a small contractor, was on a big tree-lined lot with a vast private backyard. The price was $10,000 with $1,000 down. We picked out the colors and signed the papers. I was an Ensign making in the neighborhood of $250 a month. With that salary, $10,000 was a lot of money. I tried for a veterans or GI loan. The loan officer said I did not qualify because I was not a "veteran." In the period after WWII, a veteran was someone who had been discharged from the service. I had not been

Chapter 9 Marriage, Panther Jets

discharged, therefore, I didn't qualify and we could not buy the house.

Corsair Goodbye

Bill Warwick and I wanted to see just what F4U-4 Corsair would do at altitude. We had always flown the Corsair as a fighter bomber, with bombs and rockets at low altitude, and never at high altitude as a pure fighter. So we checked out two old Corsairs and climbed to 28,000 feet using oxygen and high stage supercharger. The Corsair engine was designed to put out full takeoff horsepower up to 28,000, feet, that is, 2,800 rpm and 54 inches of manifold pressure. At 28,000 feet, we put on full power and just let them roll. Technically, the Pratt Whitney R2800 had a five-minute full power limit. However, we knew that the engine could take much more than that. Both of those old beat up Corsairs, on their fourth service tour, with rocket racks and bomb racks still attached, went 210 knots indicated airspeed, which calculated to 415 mph true airspeed. Not bad. A new Corsair, without the drag of bomb and rocket racks, would surely have gone at least 440 mph. Satisfied, Warwick and I buzzed the tower one last time. The Corsair was a great airplane and we were privileged to fly it.

Panther Jet—Hello

Our F9F-2 Panther ground school was taught by LCDR Ray Volpi and LT Dick Morrison. Both had experience in the F9F-2 Panther. We were given lectures on the engine, the hydraulic system, the control system, the speed brakes, the wheel system, the flaps, the electrical system, flight characteristics and a brand-new item to us, the ejection seat. We were given written tests on the various systems, sent to

CHAPTER 9   MARRIAGE, PANTHER JETS

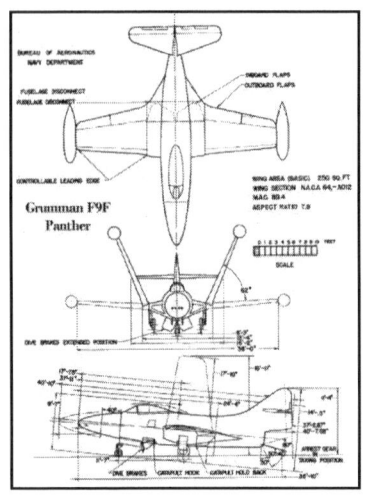

Grumman F9F-2 Panther

Alameda Naval Air Station for ejection seat training and low-pressure chamber training. After a blindfold cockpit check and a taxi test, we were ready to fly. The runway at Santa Rosa was 8,000 feet long, barely adequate for the Panther.

On the appointed day, November 19, 1951, I took off on my first jet flight. The initial acceleration on the runway was slower than the Corsair, however, as I passed 100 knots, the Panther rapidly accelerated and lifted off at about 120 or 130 knots. After the gear and flaps were retracted, the Panther accelerated rapidly to climb speed, 220 knots to 250 knots. The procedure was to take off with the canopy open. After lift off, the canopy was closed. It became eerily quiet. I was used to the 2,250-horsepower Pratt Whitney in front of me. Now I had 5,200 pounds of thrust in back of me, which I couldn't hear. I climbed to altitude of 20,000 feet at full throttle. When I leveled off the Panther easily accelerated up to its limiting mach number of .82 or 8/10 the speed of sound. At that time, engineers had not solved the problem of making a fighter go faster than the speed of sound. It had been done only in experimental aircraft that were rocket powered. So we had to be very careful when pointing the Panther at the ground. It could easily exceed its design speed and destroy itself. However, we had a new device to help us. Speed brakes. These were high-drag devices that were actuated by a switch on the throttle, which deployed two large doors under the cockpit. With the speed breaks out, we could dive vertically. Since jets flew at high altitude they had a pressurized cockpit, however, we would need to wear oxygen masks at all times.

Another new experience was getting used to the Panther's hydraulically boosted controls. This took some patience. At

CHAPTER 9   MARRIAGE, PANTHER JETS   171

Grumman F9F-2 Panther

first, I had a tendency to over control. The landing of the jet was also quite different. Early jet engines accelerated very slowly from idle. We were warned not to pull the throttle back below 80% when doing our 360 degree overhead break for landing. If we did, we probably would not have the power or airspeed needed to reach the runway. The routine we were taught was to come into the break at 250 to 300 knots, break left, speed breaks out, power 85% rpm, slowing to 225 knots, drop the gear, drop the flaps at 175 knots, slow to 130 knots at the 180-degree position, 120 to 115 knots on final.

Stopping the jet was a new experience too. In the Corsair we seldom used brakes to stop. With the Panther, I had to start breaking immediately and I used most of the runway. It was a little unnerving at first. The brakes were boosted and were not anti-lock brakes. The tires were very high pressure and it was easy, with poor breaking technique, to blow a tire. I developed a technique of rapidly pulsating my feet alternately on the brakes, while pulling the tail down with the elevator for dynamic air breaking. This worked well for me and I used the pulsating technique on all the later jets I flew. I never blew a tire.

This was a fun time for all of us. Jets were new to everyone, even Jane and the other wives came out to watch their husbands fly the jets for the first time. The Grumman built, F9F-2 Panther Jet was a tough and reliable fighter. I quickly gained confidence and affection for the Panther.

Ensign Gene Moeller

Fighter Squadron 24 was the only squadron in Air Group receiving jets. The other squadrons were intensively training in their Corsairs. I knew many of the Air Wing pilots from

Chapter 9   Marriage, Panther Jets

flight training and our combat. Losses in any squadron were sorely felt throughout the Air Wing. Jane and I were relaxing after dinner one evening, when we heard a Corsair's propeller over-speed. I found out what happened the next day. Gene Moeller and Buck Bustard of Fighter Squadron 63 were night flying when Gene noticed he had low oil pressure. He declared an emergency and returned to Santa Rosa air station. Buck told Gene to take it straight in. Gene said, "No, I'll take it into the break." This turned out to be a fatal mistake. On the downwind, his oil pressure went to zero. That's when Jane and I heard the prop wind up, then his engine quit. Gene miraculously landed the big Corsair at night in someone's backyard in Santa Rosa. Unfortunately, he neglected to raise his landing gear. The Corsair flipped on its back and slid backwards jamming dirt into the cockpit. Everyone from the BOQ tried to lift the Corsair, but it was too heavy. The cranes that tried to get into the backyard were mired down in mud. Gene suffocated.

Alameda/El Centro

October and November went rapidly. The squadron was flying night and day getting ready for the next deployment to Korea. In addition, we were sent to a special school for jet instrument training in Alameda, driving back and forth forty or fifty miles each way, every day. A very long day.

Next, we deployed to El Centro, California, for two weeks of weapons training, bombing, rockets aerial gunnery and field carrier training. We were building up flight time rapidly. Most days we were flying two flights. Jane was learning that Navy life required frequent separations from her husband.

My confidence in the F9F-2 was growing rapidly. It was strong, solid and predictable. The gun system was terrific. It had four 20 mm cannons in the nose with a lead computing gun sight. These four 20 mm cannons had a terrific punch. It had three times the range of the 50-caliber in the Corsair and had high explosive shells. I was already planning my revenge on the 37 mm flak sites in Korea.

Chapter 9 Marriage, Panther Jets

Carrier Qualifications

Four F9F-2 Panthers prepare to come aboard USS Boxer

In December, we conducted carrier qualifications on the USS Boxer off of San Diego. The F9F-2 proved to be a good carrier airplane. The big advantage we had in the Panther over the Corsair was visibility. You could see the carrier deck during the full approach. The disadvantage was that we came aboard 25 to 35 knots faster than the Corsair. We were landing on a straight deck carrier. If you made a mistake you were going to hit something very hard with nothing in front of you. In the Corsair, the engine was in front of you, in the Panther it was behind you.

LSO gives F9F-2 "Cut"

I just concentrated on making the best approach and landing I could. I quickly completed the required 14 landings, with no wave offs. I liked the Panther. We would get along very well together.

NAAS Fallon, Nevada, LCDR Conklin/LCDR Jernigan

The squadron made one final weapons training deployment to Fallon, Nevada, in January 1952, in preparation for our deployment to Korea on USS Boxer in February. It was a good deployment where we developed tactics that we would use in Korea. I was feeling very confident in the airplane and asked the XO if I could I do a victory roll break on return

Chapter 9   Marriage, Panther Jets

Victory Roll Break at Fallon

of our final training flight. He said OK and I include here a picture taken by our maintenance crew when I returned.

The weather was very unsettled when we were preparing to return to Santa Rosa. We were scheduled in flights of two. I was scheduled to lead ENS Pooley Wood. The skipper, LCDR Conklin, would lead LT Trinkle.

LCDR Conklin gave me the option of filing an instrument flight plan or returning by visual flight rules. I opted for the latter. I led ENS Wood underneath the weather, dodging rain showers and mountains, without much difficulty. ENS Wood and I landed in Santa Rosa in less than an hour. We had just landed when the Duty Officer received word that Skipper Conklin had lost control on instruments. He had gone straight into the mountains at high speed and had been killed. LT Trinkle narrowly missed the same fate. He was able to pull out with just feet to spare.

We had the standard memorial service. Very sad. This was a hard blow to the squadron. Our new Commanding Officer was dead only weeks before we were to return to combat. LCDR Jernigan on the Air Wing staff was ordered into VF-24 as our new Commanding Officer. There was no ceremony.

LCDR Jernigan would prove to be a strong and capable combat leader.

Awards

Before Air Group Two departed NAAS Santa Rosa, we all dressed up for a formal inspection. Captain Marineo, Commander Fleet Air Alameda, traveled to Santa Rosa to present awards for the Air Group's 1950-51 Korean combat on USS Boxer, USS Valley Forge and USS Philippine Sea. We

Chapter 9 Marriage, Panther Jets 175

Air Medal awards Santa Rosa January 1952

had fought aggressively with valor and sustained significant losses. However, awards were modest. Air Medals were the order of the day. Only the Air Wing Commander received a Distinguished Flying Cross. It was that kind of war.

Last Leave, Back to War

In late January 1952, I took a few days leave so Jane and I could be together before my deployment to Korea. We took our 1950 Ford and headed south toward Los Angeles. I wanted Jane to meet the Leue' side of the family. We took Floppy.

It was a fun trip and we stopped along the way to visit with my father's second cousin, Edna Lade. On arrival, Floppy leaped up, grabbing a pair of silk stockings from Edna's hand. Nice entrance!

Jane and I stayed with Edna one night, then spent another two nights with my Uncle Carl and Aunt Hazel in Huntington Beach. Carl had built a nice cozy house on Beach Boulevard. We enjoyed learning about all the innovations that he had incorporated into their home. He had a wonderful garden with all kinds of squash and other vegetables. Carl also proudly showed us their Servel, a gas refrigerator. (It lasted

Chapter 9   Marriage, Panther Jets

Jane and Floppy

for at least 40 years). They took us to Knott's Berry Farm, the Disneyland of the day, which was great fun. The weather was wonderful during this whole time. I recall how proud I was of Jane.

Our trip was over too soon. Within the first week of February 1952, the squadron moved to Alameda Naval Air Station in preparation for the move aboard USS Boxer. Jane and I stayed in one of the temporary Quonset huts that were available at NAS Alameda. These Quonset huts were fully equipped with bedding, china and everything that we needed. The price was also right. Free.

February 7, 1952. We waved as the USS Boxer was pushed into the stream by six Navy tugs. It was a slow affair pushing the big ship away from the pier and turning its bow until it was heading fair, toward the channel, the Bay Bridge, the Golden Gate Bridge, the vast Pacific and Korea. I watched Jane until she was just a speck, then she was gone. We would not see each other for nine months. We wrote every day.

Jane had arranged to room with Vi Vieli, Lieutenant Jack Vieli's wife and Helen Radtke, Herman Radtke's wife. Jane found a nursing job at Santa Rosa hospital. She would be with friends and had a job. Still, this was a big test for her. We had been married only seven months. She was very young and on her own for the first time in her life. She would prove to be tough, weathering the difficulties of being on her own very well. She would learn what it was to be a "Navy Wife." A very difficult assignment, but she would pass with flying colors.

Chapter Ten

USS Boxer, 1952

Fighting China

February 14, 1952. En route to Korea, Air Group Two was once again aboard USS Boxer, conducting training in the Hawaiian Islands. We spent several days doing extensive air operations, bombing, strafing and tactics. We also sharpened our skills at carrier launches and landings. Unfortunately, during this training, Lieutenant Trinkle, attempting to land late in the afternoon, looking into the setting sun, flew into the Boxer's ramp and was killed. Ironically, Trinkle, a VO/VS Cruiser float plane pilot of WWII fame, had recently escaped death when our late Skipper

Fighter Squadron 24 Officers on board the USS Boxer, CV-21,

Conklin flew into the ground returning from Fallon, Nevada.

We had one last liberty in Waikiki, then headed west for combat. In spite of our recent losses, the squadron remained a close and confident group. We had learned to cope with adversity. Many of the new squadron officers who

CHAPTER 10   USS BOXER, 1952   178

LCDR Bill Jernigan Commanding Officer VF-24, 1952

had joined the squadron in Santa Rosa came aboard with strong Naval Air backgrounds. LCDR Joe Pace, our new Executive Officer, was a steady, low-key and experienced fighter pilot; LCDR Ray Volpi, our Operations Officer, brought WWII fighter experience; Lieutenant Fred Nevett would prove to be a strong, jovial and steady Division leader; and LTJG Dick Morrison, brought needed jet experience. We were blessed with two of the best non-flying Maintenance and Intelligence Officers in the fleet, LCDR Jack Vieli and LT Dick Maxwell USNR. Maxwell, a practicing lawyer, was called to active duty for the Korean War.

Our new Skipper, LCDR Bill Jernigan, quickly exerted his strong, confident leadership style preparing the squadron for our new combat role. His mantra was, "Never assume anything." As professional naval aviators, we were eager to try our skills with our new Panther Jet aircraft. We knew we would not be carrying as much heavy ordnance and staying on station for long periods of time, or flying close air support for Marines, as we had with the Corsair. However, with the Panther's superior gun system and performance we looked forward to attacking enemy gun positions in our flak suppression role. We might even get a chance to go against the Mig fighters.

Chapter 10 USS Boxer 1952 179
Combat, Jet Aircraft and Straight Carrier Decks

Flying the Panther in combat introduced a whole new set of challenges. Our missions were now scheduled for only one and a half hours, half of the Corsair mission time. Our fuel was limited. Since there was no in-flight refueling we had only one place to land safely: the USS Boxer. We did have a new and improved navigation device for finding the ship. It was the ADF or Automatic Direction Finder. When tuned to the Boxer's low-frequency homer, a needle in our cockpit pointed to the ship. We still had YG/ZB as a backup.

Navigation over the beach was now much more challenging; we only had maps for guidance, as before, but we were moving much faster. We couldn't afford to get lost in the rugged Korean landscape, as we did occasionally in the Corsair. This meant, if the weather was bad, as it frequently was, there was no margin for error. There simply was no extra time or fuel to wait out bad weather or divert to someplace else. We planned to have 1,000 pounds of fuel upon retuning to the ship to land. This would give us, at most, two attempts to land without running out of fuel. Any delay, such as a flight deck crash, would put us in the water. Our objective was to get aboard the first pass and get out of the arresting gear expeditiously, so our shipmates following could also get aboard.

Most pilots agreed, the Panther was actually easier for us to bring aboard than the Corsair. We could see the LSO and the ship clearly without making the tight turning approach necessitated by the Corsair's long nose. Also, the jet had no torque to counter when changing power. The down side of the Panther was, it came aboard 25-35 knots faster than the Corsair and throttle response was much slower. You could get in trouble faster and the consequences were more severe. Our carrier landings were still controlled by the Landing Signal Officer with paddles. We were still landing straight up the deck, the angled deck carrier had not been invented. If we missed the arresting wires, we were going to hit something... hard.

CHAPTER 10   USS BOXER   1952   180

To preclude as much mayhem as possible, a series of barriers had been designed to stop a jet that missed the

LCDR Ray Volpi, Fighter Squadron 24 Operations Officer, briefs a strike

arresting wires. The first of these was the "Davis" barrier. The Davis was a low, 2-foot-high nylon strap that was designed to catch the nose wheel, which then pulled the arresting wire up into the jet's main mounts (wheel struts), which should arrest the jet with minor damage. There were two or three Davis barriers. If the jet was too high to actuate the Davis barriers, next up the deck was a 10-to-12 foot high nylon "Barricade" attached to the last arresting wire. The nylon Barricade was a last-ditch device that would damage the jet extensively and could injure or kill the pilot, but was the last means to prevent catastrophic damage to all the aircraft and crewman up forward on the bow. Our squadron was to experience both Davis barrier and nylon Barricade arrestments.

VF-24 Flight Organization

We usually flew in groups of four, called "divisions." LCDR Ray Volpi was my division leader, LT Bruce Robinson was section leader, Ensign Duke Dudek and I were wingmen. This was a strong, well-balanced group. Ray Volpi had been a fighter pilot in WWII, the only pilot in our squadron with

CHAPTER 10   USS BOXER   1952   181

WWII fighter combat experience. He was a confident and aggressive fighter pilot. I was to learn a lot from him. Bruce Robinson had Corsair combat experience with us on the Boxer, Valley Forge and Phil Sea cruises. He was steady and intelligent with a great sense of humor. Duke Dudek was on his first cruise. We roomed together in the JO bunkroom. We shared common interests and skills and were both newly married. Volpi's division had trained together in Santa Rosa and we developed into a strong aggressive team in combat. We were superior around the ship. (Dudek and I both flew the entire Boxer cruise without a wave off, always getting aboard the first pass).

Ray Volpi, Mick Rooney, Dave Leue', Tim Timidaiski

Administrative Duties

My administrative duties aboard ship were several. I remained the Squadron Assistant Flight Officer, in charge of preparing the fight schedule for the following day's combat. It required I study the Air Plan for the next day's missions and make out the rough schedule each day after the evening meal. This was movie time in the Wardroom. Since I was not a movie lover, I fit well in this job.

I was also the squadron First Lieutenant in charge of insuring the VF-24 assigned spaces were maintained to high standards. In this duty, I worked with the squadron Leading Chief Petty Officer inspecting spaces and forming working

Chapter 10   USS Boxer   1952   182

parties to paint, clean or otherwise keep squadron spaces "shipshape."

My third assignment was as squadron Enlisted Training Officer. This duty required that I procure the required Naval Training publications and provide training for the various squadron enlisted Rates to insure they were competitive in the periodic fleet-wide enlisted promotion examinations. This duty was an introduction to the rules, regulations and bureaucracy of the Navy promotion system. I had much to learn.

First Combat in the Panther

My logbook shows I flew 20 missions in April. Several of these missions were strike missions. On strike missions, we escorted large groups of Corsairs and Sky Raiders against hard, well-defended targets such as bridges, rail yards or large military installations. On these missions, the Panther Jets acted as flak suppressors. We usually carried four 250-pound or six 100-pound fragmentation bombs with VT fusing

Eight VF-24 Panthers forward on the port bow of USS Boxer following a strike,

(air burst). En route to the target, we would fly above the strike aircraft, weaving, then approaching the target, roll on our backs and dive through the bombers to hit the known flak sites with our bombs, as the bombers commenced their dives. We would then pull vertically to use our speed to zoom to 8,000 or 10,000 feet, then roll on our backs and dive again strafing with our 20 mm cannon to cover the bombers as they pulled off the target. It was an effective tactic.

I loved it when LCDR Volpi, hearing the strike leader's call,

A VF-24 Panther takes a wave off, Sea of Japan off Korea

"Xray," the signal to commence the attack, rolled the division on our backs at 12,000 feet, diving vertically through the strike group toward our flak sites with guns blazing.

The squadron lost our first aircraft and pilot in April when LT Jack Griffith of the Air Wing staff, did not return from a photo escort mission. Also, during this month, Ensign Duke Dudek was hit in his wing tank but returned safely. In general, because of the Panther's speed, we were not hit as often as we had been in the Corsair.

Killing a Flak Site

In our three previous combat cruises flying Corsairs, we had lost many of our closest friends from well-aimed, concentrated, anti-aircraft artillery fire. Now we had an aircraft and gun system that could even the score.

The enemy guns, Russian or Chinese, rapid-fire 37-mm, 57-mm or crew-served 85-mm, were usually well camouflaged and difficult to see. Often, to hide their location, these sites would not open up or shoot until we passed or had began our pullout from our dive. Then, red balls of fire or tracers or bursting flak, would fly by from our six o'clock (rear). As number four in our division, I was the recipient of the majority of this flak.

Chapter 10   USS Boxer 1952   184

During briefing one day, I suggested to LCDR Volpi, "If after a run or a dive, when we are in trail, and I see red balls of fire and see the flak site, I'll say, 'I've got one.' If you say, 'OK,' I will pull up vertically, converting my speed to altitude, then go over the top on my back, put my nose down looking for the smoke and dust always kicked up by the firing guns. The flight can follow in reverse order, hammering the flak guns." LCDR Volpi approved this tactic.

On a reconnaissance mission shortly thereafter, a site of several 37 mm opened up on me as I pulled out of a dive. I called, "I got one." Volpi said, "OK." As planned, I looped to 10,000 feet, pulled back my throttle, put out my speed brakes, pointing straight down. I put my gun sight on the flak guns. I fired several short one-second bursts, covering the flak guns with high explosive incendiary shells. As I began my pullout I saw tracers coming from a supporting 12.7 mm machine gun slightly off to my left. I kicked left rudder to put my nose on that site too, but before I could get him in my sights, the machine gunner hit my aircraft. Wham! My guns stopped firing.

VF-24 F9F-2 Panther taxis forward after recovery USS Boxer 1952

When I returned to the USS Boxer and landed, the maintenance crew found a hole in my aircraft's nose made by an armor-piercing 12.7 mm round. The round had traveled

Chapter 10   USS Boxer   1952

VF-24 Skipper's aircraft "hawks" the deck for landing

through the gun bay, hit my gun control solenoid, stopping my guns. This saved the machine gunner's life. His 12.7 mm armor-piercing round was stopped by the armor plate, just in front of me. Without the armor plate, the round would have hit me somewhere below the waist, every warrior's nightmare. At the time I had no children. I carried this armor piercing round with me for many years, keeping it on my dresser with cuff links etc. Unfortunately, this memento was stolen with other personal effects, such as my sword, pieces of North Korean rock picked from my wings, etc., when thieves broke into our house in Vista, California. A more lasting memento is my family, an ever growing cast of characters. Thank you, Lord!

Grounded

I loved to strafe in the Panther. The F9F-2 Panther's gun system was reliable, powerful and accurate. The 20 mm HEI (high-explosive incendiary) rounds seemed to annihilate everything they hit. I had confidence that I could hit and destroy any enemy gun emplacement, truck or suitable gun target that I saw. Still, we had lost too many aircraft going low. Air Wing rules were developed setting 1,000 feet as the minimum altitude for attacks. This essentially ruled out strafing many targets, since we had to go lower than a 1,000 feet to see and attack these smaller targets with guns. Our aircraft had 16 mm movie gun cameras, which took movies when we pulled the trigger or pushed the bomb pickle. This recorded all of our bombing or strafing runs. These gun camera films were developed after flying each day and shown before the movie in the Wardroom after the evening meal. I never stayed for the gun camera films or the movie,

ENS Pooley Wood, ENS Sandy Sunstrom and LTJG Dick Morrison

since I was always in to our squadron Ready Room making out the fight schedule for the following day's missions.

One evening, I was deep in this process when I got a call from Ensign Pooley Wood, a fellow VF-24 pilot. Pooley said in a low voice, "Louie, you better hide, the Air Wing Commander and Skipper Jernigan just saw your terrific gun camera film. They are hopping mad!"

Earlier that day, the flight leader for our road reconnaissance mission was grounded due to a cold. This flight, now all Ensigns, was led by Sandy Sunstrom. All of us young guys loved to strafe, so we agreed to pull our gun camera circuit breakers, to prevent taking movies of our low-level attacks.

On this mission, I conducted a low-level strafing attack on a railroad yard, hitting train cars, the station and finally an "on the deck" attack on the railroad water tower. I obliterated

CHAPTER 10   USS BOXER 1952   187

the water tower in a hail of 20mm fire. The water tower seemed to fill my windscreen at the end of my run. It made a spectacular movie. I had neglected to pull my circuit breaker.

Of course, I could not hide. Later Skipper Jernigan called me into his state room and informed me my strafing was great, but he had to ground me.

I said my "Mea Culpa" and rested for two days.

In "The Drink"

Another significant change in our carrier operations with the F9F-2 Panther Jet was the method of launching. All jets had to be catapulted to get safely airborne. Jets could not launch by a deck run as the Corsair. The hydraulic catapults on the Boxer, and its WWII sister ships, were not designed for jets. They were designed for launching propeller aircraft. They were also brutally rough. The shot was like being rear-ended at a stoplight. The Boxer catapults were the roughest of any catapults I experienced in 30-plus years of service.

The Boxer H4 hydraulic catapults had been modified to 4000 pounds of pressure to give them enough end speed for launching the Panther, but this was still only 85 knots. Thus, if there was little or no wind, the ship needed to steam at least 30 knots to provide sufficient wind over the deck to gain the 115 knots minimum flying speed required by the Panther. Modern steam catapults are designed to give end speeds of 150 knots for launching jets even at low wind speeds. We had no such luxury. On every Boxer jet launch, if the first jets settled off the bow, indicating not enough wind over the deck, the Air Boss would proclaim, "Take two bombs off the jets," then they would continue launching.

Early in the cruise, I had watched an F9F-2 settle into the water off the bow of the carrier operating alongside us. I had wondered, "How did that happen?" I was to find out.

In May, we flew only eight missions because of weather. At this point I had become very confident, too confident. On the 25th of May, we were launching an all out strike. The targets

CHAPTER 10 USS BOXER 1952

were military installations in Pyongyang, the capital of North Korea. I was carrying six 250-pound fragmentation bombs for flak suppression. There was no wind. LCDR Volpi and I were the first two jets on the catapults. Duke Dudek, who was grounded because of a cold, was standing between the catapults, next to the cat officer, watching the launch. He waved to me as I pulled onto the port cat. The Cat Officer tensioned Volpi on the starboard catapult and then me on the port cat. The Cat Officer took our salutes together, then launched Volpi first, then me. Bang, Bang.

Immediately after I was catapulted I snapped my gear up, made a smart clearing turn (a mistake). My Panther stalled. The nose dropped to the right, then I hit Ray Volpi's slipstream. This put me deeper into a stall. The airplane buffeted. I dropped the nose slightly to keep flying speed and fought to keep the wings level. I eased the nose up as I settled into the water, wings level, nose up.

I hit with a good jolt. I did not un-strap immediately. The Panther skipped three times. The jolts were significant, but less than I expected. I was doing about 115 knots (130 mph) when I hit the water. The aircraft floated briefly. The nose fairing covering the guns was gone, otherwise, it was intact. I tried to stand up, but got tangled in my straps, so I just sat

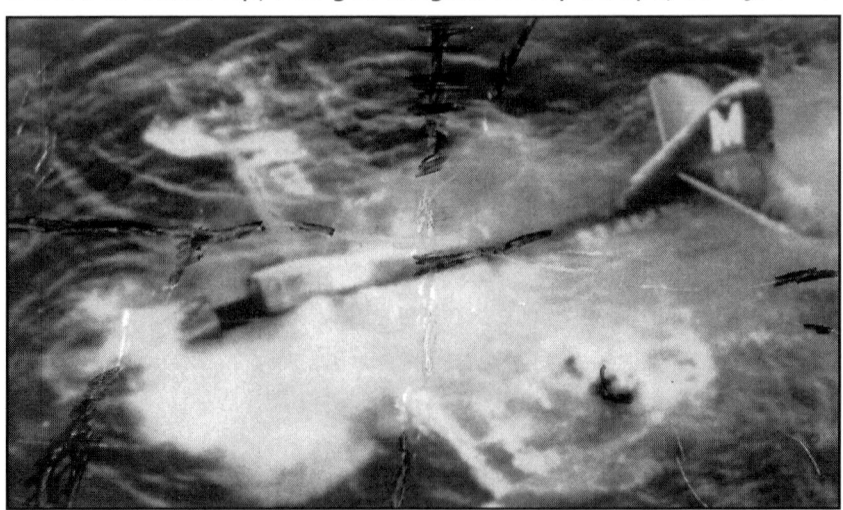

Ensign David Leue', May 25,1952, Sea of Japan,

down and slowly un-strapped, then went over the left side with my chute and life raft underneath me. I knew I had gone in right in front of the ship. The ship's captain had witnessed the crash, turned the Boxer port (left). The ship passed about 50 ft. to my left. I tried to wave, indicating I was OK, but my buoyant seat pack with the life raft kept tipping me over.

After the ship passed, the plane guard helicopter came over me with the crewmen pointing to the sign underneath, "Remove Chute." I un-strapped my chest strap and my leg straps. I assumed I was free of the chute. However, I was unaware the parachute straps were still around my shoulders. I may have been dazed. The crewman kept pointing at the sign, but I thought I was free of the chute. I was not. Finally, with the ship charging over the horizon at 30 knots launching aircraft, the helo crewman decided to lower the horse collar and pick me up, chute and all. This was very dangerous for the helicopter; if my chute popped out, it would pull the helicopter and all of us into the sea. I stood outside the helo on the step all the way back to the ship with my chute pack hanging off me. There was no room inside for me in the old H03S. The helo pilot was justifiably unhappy about having to pick me up with my chute. I thanked him and bought him a bottle of whiskey next time in port. Once back aboard, the medics checked me over in sickbay and gave me a shot of whiskey. I only had a stiff neck and they sent me back to duty. I flew a photo escort mission the next day.

Stan Henderson

My friendship with Stan Henderson went all the way back to Pre-Flight. We became good friends in flight training, then had gone to different squadrons, but had retained a mutual respect. He was from Miami, and had come into the Navy under the V-5 program out of high school with flight training as a Midshipman, as I had. He was in the close group that I trained with in Corsairs at Cabaniss Field, Texas: Johnny Thompson, Herman Radtke, Bob Wallin, Ned Steiner, and Bernie Shank. He was big, sandy haired, low-key, and

CHAPTER 10   USS BOXER   1952   190

Stan Henderson

smooth talking, with a nice sense of humor. He was a superior aviator and warrior. A tough guy with a big heart. Flying Corsairs in VF-64, our sister squadron, he had made all three of our combat cruises, and was so far unscathed.

The odds caught up with him on a road reconnaissance mission just inland along the east coast of Korea. They hit him in the neck with automatic weapons or a fragment of a flak burst. Bleeding profusely from his jugular vein, he turned out to sea. Realizing he would not last long enough to make the ship, he spotted a US destroyer doing shore bombardment. His wingman contacted the ship. Stan landed his Corsair alongside the destroyer in the sea. The destroyer Captain launched a whale boat, and rescued him. This was his ticket home. Jane later mentioned in a letter that Stan was back in Santa Rosa and doing well.

John "Kor-day" Kordeleski

John Kordeleski

John Kordeleski was big, jovial and Polish. He was almost too nice a guy to be a fighter pilot. Our friendship went back to Pre-Flight, Pensacola and Advanced training in Corsairs at Cabaniss Field, Texas. He always had a nice new car. I recall the wild ride in his new 1949 Mercury, racing Johnny Thomson in his new Dodge, through the Texas plains, from Cabaniss to Pensacola, for Carrier Qualification. We had shared the chaos of the JO bunkroom with forty Ensigns on Valley Forge and Philippine Sea. He good naturedly put up with the harassment of our fellow pilots as he designed and together we painted the fine Air Group

CHAPTER 10   USS BOXER   1952

Two plaque presented to USS Valley Forge in 1951. John was a member of Fighter Squadron 64, still doing the tough work in F4U-4 Corsairs, as he had done so well on Boxer, Valley Forge and Philippine Sea.

In May, Kor-day's luck ran out. Flying his hundredth mission, his flight was called in to assist in the rescue of a downed Air Force B-26 crew. The Chinese shot him down and killed him. He still lays on the North Korean hill where he fell at age 24.

Boxer Fire

June was another busy month. I flew eighteen missions, a mixture of armed reconnaissance, strike and combat air patrol. On combat air patrol missions we were stationed at 20,000 feet between the task force and the beach, ready to intercept any hostile aircraft. This never happened, but it was a requirement that was performed on a daily basis. The task force consisted of two to four carriers with supporting destroyers and cruisers for protection against enemy submarines, surface ships or aircraft. Our task force was never attacked, but this effort had to be made nevertheless.

July 6, 1952. I got up early in preparation for a morning combat air patrol (CAP) mission. VF-24's Ready Room One was just under the flight deck on the portside, amidships. Just forward of the Ready Room was an officer's head. After briefing with Lieutenant Commander Volpi's flight, I went forward to the head before the flight. When I opened the hatch to the head, I was surprised to see there was about 6 inches of water sloshing on the deck. A commode had overflowed. I was the squadron First Lieutenant, the officer in charge of keeping the spaces working, so it was my task to find someone to fix it.

I was about to go back to the Ready Room to call the squadron Leading Chief for some crewman to fix the head, when the ships PA system announced, "Fire! Fire! On the hangar deck, frame 117. This is no drill! Fire! Fire!"

Chapter 10   USS Boxer 1952

I didn't pay any attention. We heard fire alarms all hours of day and night on the ship. When I finally opened the hatch, I was faced with a solid black wall of smoke. I couldn't see six inches. I felt my way aft and opened the hatch to the Ready Room. I hollered "Fire, Fire!" The pilots in Ready Room were ignoring the alarm as I had. The black smoke pouring in around me convinced them and they ran for the exits.

I retraced my steps through the black smoke, feeling my way to the catwalk and the flight deck. When I burst out into the sunshine, there was a solid wall of smoke and flame below me shooting from the elevator opening to the hangar deck. I

USS Boxer CV-21 burns July 6, 1952, Sea of Japan off of Korea

could hear machine guns firing. They were cooking off in the planes burning on the hangar deck just below me.

I ran forward in the port catwalk then down the ladder to the hangar deck to get to the junior officers bunkroom, just forward of the hangar deck. Machine gun rounds from burning aircraft were ricocheting around the hangar deck as I ran through it. Previously, on other ships, I had noticed patched bullet holes on the JO bunkroom bulkhead from similar incidents.

Chapter 10 USS Boxer 1952

Now, I worried the machine guns firing behind me would go through the bunkroom bulkhead and kill my sleeping buddies. I ran into the bunk room yelling "Fire, Fire, this is no drill!!" It was dark, I turned on the lights, which provoked a smattering of profanity. I again yelled, "Fire! Fire! Wake up! Get out! This is no drill. The ship is on Fire!" I pulled sleeping forms out of the rows of three-high bunks. Some thought it was a joke and swung at me as I pulled them to the deck.

I retraced my steps through the machine gun bullets and chaos on the hangar deck, going top side on the flight deck. There I joined working parties taking bombs off the strike aircraft, rolling them to the catwalks and throwing them over the side. At about this time, a horrendous explosion on the hangar deck wracked the ship. A 500-pound bomb on one of the Corsairs, blew up from the heat, killing an entire Marine fire party, wrecking the hangar deck and setting dozens of aircraft on fire. There was a call for volunteers to man hoses on the hangar deck. I went below, joined a hose crew fighting fires that had spread to the aircraft and the wiring in the overhead of the hangar bay. Many dropped off of the hose crews from the heat and exhaustion while others joined. I took over one hose crew. Many of us fought the fires for four hours before they were finally brought under control.

Our squadron lost our flight surgeon, Dr. Shopshire, and our Corpsman, both died in their aid station on the hangar deck. The air wing and ship lost many others from the smoke, fire and explosions.

Sixty-three sailors on the hangar deck and berthing compartments aft, went over the side into the sea to escape the smoke and flames. Amazingly, all who went over the side were recovered by task force ships.

The initial fire was caused by two squadron ordnance men, who improperly disarmed a F4U-5 (N) Corsair night fighter. While disarming the guns they inadvertently fired several 20 mm HEI rounds into the Corsair ahead. The Corsair blew up.

CHAPTER 10   USS BOXER 1952   194

Pete & David Maugans

This fire started on the hangar deck, just below where I was standing in the head above.

There were many stories of heroic acts and rescues. LT Tim Timidaiski, a VF-24 pilot, donned an OBA, Oxygen Breathing Apparatus (he had been trained during earlier destroyer experience) then plunged into smoke-filled compartments to save trapped crewmen. He later received the Navy Commendation Medal.

Two shipmates, brothers, Pete and David Maugans, sailors in Fighter Squadron 63, had very harrowing experiences during the Boxer fire. A hometown newspaper article, based on a letter to their mother, is priceless. I include it here:

"THE DAILY MAIL, HAGERSTOWN, MD, AUGUST 18, 1952"

Sharpsburg Sailor Rescued From Sea After Jet Explodes

On Aircraft Carrier Boxer

"Just a little over a week ago the story had appeared in newspapers of the explosion of a jet plane aboard the carrier, killing nine of the Boxer's crew members and injuring 75 others.

The Maugans brothers, Edward 'Pete', a second class petty officer, and David Allen 'Gig,' naval airman, were both uninjured in the calamity at sea, but Pete had been one of the 63 crew members who were forced to leap overboard to escape the flames.

In a letter to his parents, Pete described the panic and confusion that reigned aboard the Boxer as the men fled from the spreading flames, not knowing the actual location of the fire nor any safe exit to escape it and the dense smoke. He also told of the uncertainty and fear that gripped him as he waited to find out whether or not his brother had escaped injury. As he later found out, however, it was Gig who had the real reason to worry, since Pete's name had been mistakenly omitted from the list of those picked up out of the ocean by the destroyer "Stembel," and Gig feared that he had been lost at sea.

Pete's very complete account of the sea-borne terror started with his hearing "Fire Quarters" sounded at about 6:30 on that fateful morning, July 6th. At the time he was in the crew's living quarters one deck below the hangar deck. Shortly after the word was passed that there was a fire at frame 117, he heard the machine gun bullets going off "like a big popcorn machine"— and in seconds the compartment was filled with smoke.

The fire had started when a returning night fighter had somehow fired a round of ammo by mistake on the hangar, and flames leaped to the planes and stored ammunition. Pete didn't know this at the time, however. All he knew was that he was trapped below-decks and the ventilating system was pouring heat and smoke into the compartments below the hangar deck.

To escape the smoke, Pete and several buddies headed for the latrine. They had all tried to find a hatch open to the upper deck, unsuccessfully, and were sure they were trapped. The smoke kept getting thicker, to the point that to breathe, Pete had to take off his undershirt and soaked it in water to hold over his face. Maugans said one of the mates encouraged the men to pray for help and was unsure of what to say and was told to ask the Lord to come help them or send his Son, Jesus, to help them. What thundered through that compartment of the ship came out loud and clear: "Lord, come help me now, don't send your Son, this ain't no place for a kid," and with those words the hatch opened.

It was almost as smoky out on deck; they soon found, because a bomb-laden plane exploded adding its lethal cargo

CHAPTER 10   USS BOXER 1952   196

to the holocaust, setting off several more gas tanks. Pete and the other crewmen huddled in a boat pocket on the hangar deck level...waiting.

"It really got hot then," Pete wrote in his letter. "And when that bomb went off it blew an empty belly tank down into the boat pocket on top of us. I was the farthest away from the flames, but I could feel the heat on my back as if I were afire. The smoke kept pouring out so thick I couldn't see my hands before my face, and so acrid that my eyes burned and I could barely breathe.

"Then someone in the back started yelling that he was getting burned and we all knew what we would have to do. It had been inevitable all along, but no one wants to jump overboard unless he really has to."

It was risky jumping the 45 feet into the water, but the men had no choice. Sixty-three of them, cut off from the comparative safety of the rest of the ship, lined up and took their chances at missing the debris and bombs that were being jettisoned over the side by other crew members.)

"I hit the water like a ton of bricks," wrote Pete Maugans, "and it seemed an hour until I came back up to the surface. Then I started swimming away from the ship as fast as I could. Luckily, someone up on that ghost ship in its blanket of smoke heard us all hit the water and they threw in some life-jackets. By hanging onto the jackets and treading water we managed to stay up—and Thank Heavens the sea was calm. We weren't in the water more than half an hour before they spotted us and lowered several motor whale-boats to pick us up. It was the "USS Stembel," and altogether she picked up 32 of our men—and treated us royally."

It was more than four hours later that the fire aboard the Boxer was finally brought under control, and around 1 o'clock in the afternoon the destroyer was maneuvering to return the men to their own ship. It couldn't have been too soon for Pete, though, because he still had not seen or heard from his brother since the initial explosion—Gig having already been on duty topside helping to launch planes when the

CHAPTER 10 USS BOXER 1952 197

accident occurred. The reunion when Pete got back aboard the Boxer was worth all that both brothers had experienced in the ordeal — since neither was scratched.

The scene aboard the Boxer early that morning, however, could not have been more critical or calamitous had the damage been inflicted by the enemy. Gig later described to his brother how a bomb blew up the hangar deck near the fire just as two Marines walked onto the deck. One was blown over the side and hasn't been seen since; seven more men were found in an office between decks—or what was left of them," said Pete. Among them, he added was the doctor "who fixed my toe last November."

Eleven jets and three propeller planes were destroyed in the fire, along with offices in which metal decks and bulkheads were melted and crumbled. In closing his letter, Pete Maugans said that the Boxer was limping back to Japan for repairs."

The majority of the VF-24 Panthers, which were situated on the hangar deck, were burned beyond recognition. The ship suffered major damage. Briefly, we thought we would be sent home, but the Navy was determined that the Boxer would stay in the Far East. We sailed into Yokosuka, Japan, for emergency repairs. All hands, including aviators and officers, such as myself, turned to twenty-four hours a day on work parties. We cleaned up, rewired, straightened, welded, repaired and re-painted the ship. Japanese shipyard workers assisted with the heavy electrical and mechanical work. The squadron was issued replacement aircraft, which we painted in our colors. This work was completed in approximately three weeks. We sailed again for the sea of Japan to begin strikes against North Korea.

Suiho Raid

Our last mission of the Boxer cruise was against the Suiho power plant on the Yalu River. The front lines had stabilized along the 38th parallel in August 1952. This was where the war had begun over two years before. The feeling in Washington was that the Chinese were ready for a cease-fire

CHAPTER 10   USS BOXER   1952   198

and we should strike them with one last blow. Our government decided to hit all of the North Korean power plants at one time. Their largest hydro power plant was on the Yalu River, just 40 miles from the big Mig base, at Antung, Manchuria. There were more than 200 Mig fighters based at Antung. Up until this point, after two years of combat, no one in our air wing had even seen, let alone been threatened by a Mig.

But now, to attack the Suiho power plant, we would have to go into the Migs' backyard, just 40 miles from their base! The plan was to take 36 AD-1 Sky Raiders carrying three 2,000-pound bombs each. The Sky Raiders would be escorted by 36 F9F-2 Panthers with 36 Air Force F-86 for high cover. This required squadrons of AD-1 and F9F-2 from three aircraft carriers.

The Suiho strike on August 29, 1952 was led by our Air Wing Commander, Commander Downey. On this mission, I flew right wing on LCDR Ray Volpi. Our mission was to escort the Sky Raiders to the target then dive on the flak sites on the south side of the Yalu River. Because of the vast difference in speeds between the propeller driven Sky Raiders and our Panther Jets, we were launched 30 minutes after the Sky Raiders. We rendezvoused with the Sky Raiders about 50 miles south of the Yalu River, then flew cover over them until they rolled into their dives on the Suiho Dam power plant. The strike came off perfectly.

We dove simultaneously on our assigned flak sites firing our 20 mm. I was sure that I would see Migs. As I pulled out of my dive, Ray Volpi called frantically, "Dave, my guns are jammed, don't lose me!" I thought, "Great, if we see Migs, I'm the shooter." We pulled out low jinking and looking. Not a single Mig!

Later, we found out from Intelligence, the Chinese thought we were going to attack Antung (We should have! I fantasized about doing this on my own. What a job I could have done with those 20mm!) The Migs took off and fled

CHAPTER 10　　USS BOXER 1952　　199

Hits on the Suiho Power Plant, Yalu River August 29, 1952

deep into China. Our Sky Raiders, with great bombing, totally demolished the Suiho hydro power plant.

LCDR Ray Volpi Ray Volpi proved to be a superior combat leader, carrier pilot and a friend for life. In spite of his skill and friendship, he made one small mistake that nearly killed us both. Such are the risks of Naval Aviation.

Returning from the Suiho raid we were confronted with a task force formation of four aircraft carriers operating together in close proximity. Volpi had briefed us well about this formation and the correct procedures to be used to minimize conflicts between the air groups of each ship. Boxer would be the carrier on the starboard (right) side of the task force. On return for this recovery Boxer flights were to approach the ship from the stern until abeam the island of the Boxer, then we would turn 90 degrees right until perpendicular to the ship's course, then the flight would break up for landing by turning left 180 degrees to cross the bow ahead of the Boxer then turning 90 degrees port (left) into the downwind for recovery.

LCDR Ray Volpi

CHAPTER 10 USS BOXER 1952

Our division was the last to recover. Volpi, leading the division, received a foul deck wave off when the aircraft in front of him had trouble getting out of the gear. I followed in sequence after Robinson and Dudek. Volpi took it around again to recover last, immediately after me. I came aboard and taxied forward. The deck was jammed full with almost no space forward of the barriers. I crossed the barriers expeditiously, knowing Volpi was next to land behind me.

The taxi signalman picked me up telling me to slow down. He was in front of me directing me carefully to the port side of the deck near the catwalk. He was directing me, looking right at me. Suddenly, his eyes grew large with fear. He dove for the catwalk. The crash horn sounded, "Udell, Udell... Smash!!Crash!!" Flight deck wood and metal parts hurtled past my cockpit. Ray Volpi's Panther slammed to a stop only inches from my right wing, wrapped in nylon.

Ray had gone low on his approach and broke his hook on the ramp. His F9F-2 took the nylon barricade at 115 knots. The barricade did its job. Fortunately, the taxi signalman had directed me to the port side.

We both took off our helmets looked at each other and laughed.

This was our last combat mission of the war. USS Boxer and Air Group Two departed for Alameda, California.

We had done our duty, South Korea was still free...did the Country care?

A Different Kind of War

My shipmates and I had gone to war as very young, eager and idealistic Americans. We had been told only of Hitler's evils, none of Stalin's. Why not?

Now we were veterans, subdued by the realities of combat with the Communists, grown close, quietly confident in the knowledge we had done our duty well.

Navy Carrier Air Group Two lost approximately one third of its pilots and crew members. I witnessed true heroism daily;

however, the Air Wing received few, if any, significant awards. No matter. The country really didn't understand or care.

Make no mistake, we fought for freedom for all the Korean people. We fought for those who did not want to live under Communist rule.

More than 58,000 US/UN servicemen were killed in the Korean conflict and at least five times that number were wounded. Chinese and North Korean casualties were many times our own.

I write this book for the hundreds of thousands who fought in Korea. We fought for freedom, just as dearly as those who fought in World War II.

The South Korean people are free and prosperous today. The vestige of Stalin and his godless Communism still haunt the people of North Korea and China.

In World War II, the country had fought the Nazis and Japanese under the banner of "Unconditional Surrender." In Korea, MacArthur was fired by President Truman for proposing victory, the mantra became "Containment." We who fought, could die in that war, but victory was not allowed.

Mao's and Stalin's Communism would prove more deadly and much more robust than Hitler's fascism. For over forty years the Communist in Russia, Europe and Asia were able to control their subjects in gulags or kill them at will. Yet they always seemed to have the support of the left or progressives in the U.S.

Historians, especially those enamored with President Franklin Delano Roosevelt, have been extremely reluctant to examine FDR's role in arming Stalin thus creating the conditions that led to over forty years of Cold War with the Communists. This will be the focus of my final chapter.

CHAPTER ELEVEN

The Four Freedoms Betrayed

Looking at Korea through the Prism of Sixty Two Years

When I was young, I held President Franklin Delano Roosevelt, British Prime Minister Winston Churchill and Marshall Joseph Stalin in the highest esteem. My Korean War and Cold War experiences drove me to seriously question this view. I have spent over sixty years in research of the events that led to the Cold War. Here is my brief review:

- 1930-1933. Stalin annihilated seven to ten million Kulaks, Ukrainian farmers, who refused his forced collectivization of their farms.

- 1935-1939. Stalin carried out his "blood purges" killing tens of thousands of top Soviet military and political leaders.

Chapter 11 "Four Freedoms" Betrayed

- September 1939. Hitler <u>and</u> Stalin together opened World War II by attacking Poland. Hitler subsequently overran Poland, Belgium, France and more, while Stalin overran parts of Poland, Latvia, Lithuania and Finland. In May 1940, Stalin massacred 20,000 captured Polish officers and leaders in the Katyn forest. Documents in the U.S. National Archives reveal that both Churchill and Roosevelt positively knew of and covered up the Katyn killings.

- On January 6, 1941, before the United States was at war, President Roosevelt gave his State of the Union address to the Congress. He famously proclaimed the U.S. would have to fight "the dictators" to make the world safe for the "Four Freedoms." The Four Freedoms were: Freedom of Religion, Freedom of Expression, Freedom from Want and Freedom from Fear. See Appendix A.

- June 22, 1941, Hitler attacked his ally, the Soviet Union. At that time, Winston Churchill, said, " I would ally myself with the devil if he would fight Hitler." At the same time, our President ordered the U.S. to send "Lend – Lease" armaments to the Soviet Union, by-passing our neutrality laws.

- Five months later, after we were attacked at Pearl Harbor, President Roosevelt warmly embraced Stalin as an ally. There were no discussions with Congress or noticeable opposition in our media, Former President Hoover, alone, protested, "Roosevelt has betrayed the 'Four Freedoms.' "

- At that time, President Roosevelt had the option to tell Churchill; *Winston, I can't make that monster, Stalin, an ally. Let the Nazis and the Soviets fight each other to the death. My aim is to defeat both of those dictators, I just proclaimed this in my 'Four Freedoms speech.'*

Of course that did not happen.

Chapter 11 "Four Freedoms" Betrayed 204

I asked myself, "How could both FDR and Churchill, who had both eloquently proclaimed they would fight for freedom, ignore Stalin's 1930's annihilation of millions of his own people? How could they forgive Stalin his show trials and "blood purges" of tens of thousands. How could they ignore the recent Katyn massacre? How could they ignore the "Communist Manifesto," that promised a Communist world ?"

Churchill had grave doubts. However, embracing Stalin did not bother President Roosevelt or the American Left. Both believed Stalin was a reasonable man. Both believed that the Soviet Union's policies were "progressive," leading the way to a better world. FDR's wartime comments about Stalin and the Soviet Union clearly support this view. The American press believed Walter Duranty, New York Times reporter who was given the Pulitzer Prize for articles defending Stalin as a great man. They disbelieved Eugene Lyons, author of "Assignment in Utopia," that exposed Stalin's terror, based on his six years in the Soviet Union as a correspondent .

Prior to the war, some who knew of Stalin's terror, such as Whittaker Chambers and Walter Krivitsky, had tried to warn the President concerning Stalin and his penetration of his administration by Communist and Communist sympathizers. President Roosevelt summarily dismissed these warnings. Instead, he kept known leftists, Lauchlin Curry, his Executive Secretary, Harry Dexter White, Treasury, and Alger Hess, State Department, in extremely sensitive positions, where they were able to steer events to the advantage of Stalin throughout the war.

Recent books, *The Venona Secrets*" by Herbert Romerstein and Eric Breindel, "Sacred Secrets" by Jerrold and Leona Schecter and "*The Haunted Wood*" by Allen Weinstein and Alexander Vassiliev, all based on declassified top-secret intercepts of Soviet codes, positively prove that Lauchlin Curry, Alger Hiss and Harry

Chapter 11 "Four Freedoms" Betrayed

Dexter White were in the employ of the Communist. These works confirm these men helped undermine our very first ally, Chiang Kai-shek. At the Tehran and Yalta conferences, FDR inexplicitly ceded parts of northern China to Stalin, without consulting our ally Chiang Kai-shek.

In the last five days of WW II, Soviet armies quickly overran northern China and northern Korea. The Soviet Union then armed and equipped the Chinese Communists in northern China and thus began the "revolution" in China. Progressives in this country backed Mao Tse-tung as a reformer while denouncing Chiang Kai-shek, successor to Dr. Sun Yat-sen. Chiang had fought to unify China since 1911. The Congress of the United States subsequently cut off all aid to Chiang Kai-shek.

In 1948, the Chinese Communists, with strong Russian backing, pushed the Nationalist forces of Chiang Kai-shek, off of mainland China onto the island of Taiwan. (A peaceful, friendly, productive Taiwan exists today. Taiwan is what China could be had we backed Chiang).

The stage was set for the Korean War.

In 1949, our Secretary of State, Dean Acheson, proclaimed that Korea was no longer in our "sphere of influence." Stalin took that statement to mean we would not intervene in Korea if the Communist chose to unify Korea by force.

On June 25, 1950, the Soviet backed Communist North Korean forces of Kim Il-Sung, crossed the 38th parallel in force. The Korean War began.

By arming Stalin, Churchill and Roosevelt sentenced the world to over 40 years of war, not "cold war." The worst terror of this period was experienced by the millions living their lives behind the "Iron Curtain," with no freedoms, as described by the great Alexander Solzhenitsyn in his great works, "One Day in the Life of Ivan Denisovich" and "The Gulag Archipelago." To date I can find no major historian that has taken Franklin Delano Roosevelt and Winston

Chapter 11 "Four Freedoms" Betrayed

Churchill to task for the misery these two foisted on the world by embracing Stalin. The following histories are examples:

- "*The Battle for History, Refighting World War II,*" by John Keegan. Keegan never suggests that FDR's and Churchill's alliance with Stalin may have created the Cold War disaster that followed.

- "*Fateful Choices: The Decisions that Changed the World 1940-1941,*" by Ian Kershaw. Kershaw reviews the major early decisions of WW II entertaining many alternatives. There is no consideration that Stalin may have been as big an enemy of freedom as Hitler.

- "*What IF?:*" Essays by Stephen Ambrose, John Keegan, David McCullough, James M McPherson. None of these historians question FDR's embracing Stalin as an ally.

- "*The Cold War: A Military History*," edited by Robert Cowley, contains essays by Stephen Ambrose, Caleb Carr, Thomas Fleming, Victor Davis Hanson, David McCullough, Simon Winchester and others. Not one of them questions FDR's decision making Stalin an ally.

I believe the answer lies deep within our modern psyche, which teaches that socialism is somehow "fair" and "progressive." Despite socialism's frightful record, this theme is still deeply embedded in our major universities and mainstream press, a group that classifies itself liberal and progressive.

Our founders feared kings and queens and their abuse of power. They understood the flaws of human nature. Even as they created our great nation with limited federal powers, they worried whether it could survive mankind's dark side.

Our founders had no concept of the unbridled evil that would descend on the utopian socialist societies conceived by Marx and Engels. These progressives brought us:

Chapter 11 "Four Freedoms" Betrayed

"National Socialism" and "International Socialism," which bred:

Hitler, Stalin, Mao Tse-tung, Kim Il-sung, Ho Chi Minh, Pol Pot, Fidel Castro and other lesser despots.

Progress?

My combat experiences related in this book are offered to personalize the fight for freedom in Korea. Today the South Korean people are free and prosperous. North Korea is a socialist police state with an impoverished people. As "progressives" here in the U.S. push the country more and more toward socialist solutions, we should contemplate this history.

Our Constitution describes the most truly revolutionary, progressive government on the planet: a government by the people with powers granted by the Almighty, and freedom for all. The history of the twentieth century has amply demonstrated that changing the Constitution in the direction of big government socialism is not progress.

We must boldly teach the beauty of our Constitution, with its shared powers, limited Federal government and states rights, to all. We must expose the dismal record of big government socialism which falsely offers equality, but guarantees poverty and despotism.

The "Four Freedoms" can then safely thrive in this country and the world.

David E. Leue'

David E. Leue'

Bibliography

The Battle for History—John Keegan

Freedom Betrayed: Herbert Hoover's Secret History of the Second World War — Editor G. Nash

The Haunted Wood—Allen Weinstein & Alexander Vassiliev

The Venona Secrets: Exposing Soviet Espionage and America's Traitors — H. Romerstein

Sacred Secrets: How Soviet Intelligence Operations Changed American History—Jerrold and Leona Schecter

Winston Churchill — Christopher Catherwood

The Last Lion: Winston Spencer Churchill Alone 1932-1940 — William Manchester

The Second World War: The Gathering Storm — Winston S. Churchill

The Second World War: The Hinge of Fate — Winston S. Churchill

The Second World War: Their Finest Hour — Winston S. Churchill

The Second World War: Triumph and Tragedy — Winston S. Churchill

Winston Churchill — Robert Lewis Taylor

Churchill — Taken from the Diaries of Lord Moran — Lord Moran

Winston Churchill and His Inner Circle — John Colville

Roosevelt, The Soldier of Freedom 1940-1945 — James MacGregor Burns

The World That FDR Built: Vision and Reality — Edward Mortimer

Bibliography

Roosevelt's Secret War — Joseph E. Persico

Franklin and Winston: An Intimate Portrait of an Epic friendship — Jon Meacham

Franklin Delano Roosevelt: Champion of Freedom—Conrad Black

Roosevelt: The Lion and the Fox—James MacGregor Burns

Roosevelt & Frankfurter: Their Correspondence 1928-1945_ Max Freedman

The Conquerors— Michael Beschloss

The New Dealers — by Unofficial Observer

Lindbergh vs. Roosevelt— James P. Duffy

What If?: The World Foremost Military Historians, What Might Have Been — Editor Robert Crowley

Calls to Arms: Presidential Speeches, Messages and Declarations of War— Edited by Russell D. Buhite

The Week Before Pearl Harbor — A. A. Hoehling

Hollywood Party: How Communism Seduced the American Film Industry in the 1930-1940s — Kenneth Lloyd Billingsley

Assignment in Utopia — Eugene Lyons

Worker's Paradise: Fifty Years of Soviet Communism: A balance Sheet — Eugene Lyons

Stalin and His Hangman: The Tyrant and Those Who Killed for Him — Donald Rayfield

Stalin's Genocides — Norman M. Naimark

In Stalin's Secret Service: Memoirs of the First Soviet Master Spy — W. G. Krivitsky

The Red Decade — Eugene Lyons

Bibliography

On Borrowed Time — Leonard Mosley

Witness — Whittaker Chambers

Churchill, Hitler and The Unnecessary War — Patrick J. Buchanan

How the Far East was Lost: American Policy and the Creation of Communist China — Dr. A. Kubeck

Fateful Choices: The Decisions that Changed the World 1940-1941 — Ian Kershaw

The Cold War: A Military History — Editor by Robert Cowley

Ten Days to Destiny: The Secret Story of British Efforts to Strike a Deal with Hitler — J. Costello

Cold Friday — Whittaker Chambers

War in Korea: The Report of a Woman Combat Correspondent — Marguerite Higgins

The Bridges and TOKO-RI — James A. Michener

Edward R. Murrow: An American Original—Joseph E. Persico

Capitalism: The Unknown Ideal—Ayn Rand

The Gulag Archipelago One & Two—Alexander Solzhenitsyn

One Day in the Life of Ivan Denisovich — Alexander Solzhenitsyn

1943, The Victory That Never Was — John Grigg

The War Time Journals of Charles A. Lindbergh

History as You Heard it—Lowell Thomas

The War Years 1939-1945— Harold Nicolson

History of the Second World War — B.H. Liddell Hart

APPENDIX A FDR'S FOUR FREEDOMS SPEECH 1A

The State of the Union Speech was given by FDR January 6, 1941. At this time Hitler and Stalin were allies. Together these two dictators had attacked Poland in September 1939. Together they had overrun Europe. Stalin had already killed millions and Hitler was about to do the same.

Mr. President, Mr. Speaker, Members of the Seventy-seventh Congress:

I address you, the Members of the Seventy-seventh Congress, at a moment unprecedented in the history of the Union. I use the word "unprecedented," because at no previous time has American security been as seriously threatened from without as it is today.

Since the permanent formation of our Government under the Constitution, in 1789, most of the periods of crisis in our history have related to our domestic affairs. Fortunately, only one of these the four-year War between the States ever threatened our national unity. Today, thank God, one hundred and thirty million Americans, in forty-eight States, have forgotten points of the compass in our national unity.

It is true that prior to 1914 the United States often had been disturbed by events in other Continents. We had even engaged in two wars with European nations and in a number of undeclared wars in the West Indies, in the Mediterranean and in the Pacific for the maintenance of American rights and for the principles of peaceful commerce. But in no case had a serious threat been raised against our national safety or our continued independence.

What I seek to convey is the historic truth that the United States as a nation has at all times maintained clear, definite opposition, to any attempt to lock us in behind an ancient Chinese wall while the procession of civilization went past. Today, thinking of our children and of their children, we oppose enforced isolation for ourselves or for any other part of the Americas.

That determination of ours, extending over all these years, was proved, for example, during the quarter century of wars following the French Revolution.

While the Napoleonic struggles did threaten interests of the United States because of the French foothold in the West Indies and in Louisiana, and while we engaged in the War of 1812 to vindicate our right to peaceful trade, it is nevertheless clear that neither France nor Great Britain, nor any other nation, was aiming at domination of the whole world.

In like fashion from 1815 to 1914 ninety-nine years no single war in Europe or in Asia constituted a real threat against our future or against the future of any other American nation.

Except in the Maximilian interlude in Mexico, no foreign power sought to establish itself in this Hemisphere; and the strength of the British fleet in the Atlantic has been a friendly strength. It is still a friendly strength.

Appendix A FDR's Four Freedoms Speech 2A

Even when the World War broke out in 1914, it seemed to contain only small threat of danger to our own American future. But, as time went on, the American people began to visualize what the downfall of democratic nations might mean to our own democracy.

We need not overemphasize imperfections in the Peace of Versailles. We need not harp on failure of the democracies to deal with problems of world reconstruction. We should remember that the Peace of 1919 was far less unjust than the kind of "pacification" which began even before Munich, and which is being carried on under the new order of tyranny that seeks to spread over every continent today. The American people have unalterably set their faces against that tyranny.

Every realist knows that the democratic way of life is at this moment being' directly assailed in every part of the world assailed either by arms, or by secret spreading of poisonous propaganda by those who seek to destroy unity and promote discord in nations that are still at peace.

During sixteen long months this assault has blotted out the whole pattern of democratic life in an appalling number of independent nations, great and small. The assailants are still on the march, threatening other nations, great and small.

Therefore, as your President, performing my constitutional duty to "give to the Congress information of the state of the Union," I find it, unhappily, necessary to report that the future and the safety of our country and of our democracy are overwhelmingly involved in events far beyond our borders.

Armed defense of democratic existence is now being gallantly waged in four continents. If that defense fails, all the population and all the resources of Europe, Asia, Africa and Australasia will be dominated by the conquerors. Let us remember that the total of those populations and their resources in those four continents greatly exceeds the sum total of the population and the resources of the whole of the Western Hemisphere-many times over.

In times like these it is immature and incidentally, untrue for anybody to brag that an unprepared America, single-handed, and with one hand tied behind its back, can hold off the whole world.

No realistic American can expect from a dictator's peace international generosity, or return of true independence, or world disarmament, or freedom of expression, or freedom of religion -or even good business.

Such a peace would bring no security for us or for our neighbors. "Those, who would give up essential liberty to purchase a little temporary safety, deserve neither liberty nor safety."

APPENDIX A FDR'S FOUR FREEDOMS SPEECH 3A

As a nation, we may take pride in the fact that we are softhearted; but we cannot afford to be soft-headed.

We must always be wary of those who with sounding brass and a tinkling cymbal preach the "ism" of appeasement.

We must especially beware of that small group of selfish men who would clip the wings of the American eagle in order to feather their own nests.

I have recently pointed out how quickly the tempo of modern warfare could bring into our very midst the physical attack which we must eventually expect if the dictator nations win this war.

There is much loose talk of our immunity from immediate and direct invasion from across the seas. Obviously, as long as the British Navy retains its power, no such danger exists. Even if there were no British Navy, it is not probable that any enemy would be stupid enough to attack us by landing troops in the United States from across thousands of miles of ocean, until it had acquired strategic bases from which to operate.

But we learn much from the lessons of the past years in Europe-particularly the lesson of Norway, whose essential seaports were captured by treachery and surprise built up over a series of years.

The first phase of the invasion of this Hemisphere would not be the landing of regular troops. The necessary strategic points would be occupied by secret agents and their dupes- and great numbers of them are already here, and in Latin America.

As long as the aggressor nations maintain the offensive, they-not we will choose the time and the place and the method of their attack.

That is why the future of all the American Republics is today in serious danger.

That is why this Annual Message to the Congress is unique in our history.

That is why every member of the Executive Branch of the Government and every member of the Congress faces great responsibility and great accountability.

The need of the moment is that our actions and our policy should be devoted primarily-almost exclusively to meeting this foreign peril. For all our domestic problems are now a part of the great emergency.

Just as our national policy in internal affairs has been based upon a decent respect for the rights and the dignity of all our fellow men within our gates, so our national policy in foreign affairs has been based on a decent respect

APPENDIX A FDR'S FOUR FREEDOMS SPEECH 4A

for the rights and dignity of all nations, large and small. And the justice of morality must and will win in the end.

Our national policy is this:

First, by an impressive expression of the public will and without regard to partisanship, we are committed to all-inclusive national defense.

Second, by an impressive expression of the public will and without regard to partisanship, we are committed to full support of all those resolute peoples, everywhere, who are resisting aggression and are thereby keeping war away from our Hemisphere. By this support, we express our determination that the democratic cause shall prevail; and we strengthen the defense and the security of our own nation.

Third, by an impressive expression of the public will and without regard to partisanship, we are committed to the proposition that principles of morality and considerations for our own security will never permit us to acquiesce in a peace dictated by aggressors and sponsored by appeasers. We know that enduring peace cannot be bought at the cost of other people's freedom.

In the recent national election there was no substantial difference between the two great parties in respect to that national policy. No issue was fought out on this line before the American electorate. Today it is abundantly evident that American citizens everywhere are demanding and supporting speedy and complete action in recognition of obvious danger.

Therefore, the immediate need is a swift and driving increase in our armament production.

Leaders of industry and labor have responded to our summons. Goals of speed have been set. In some cases these goals are being reached ahead of time; in some cases we are on schedule; in other cases there are slight but not serious delays; and in some cases and I am sorry to say very important cases we are all concerned by the slowness of the accomplishment of our plans.

The Army and Navy, however, have made substantial progress during the past year. Actual experience is improving and speeding up our methods of production with every passing day. And today's best is not good enough for tomorrow.

I am not satisfied with the progress thus far made. The men in charge of the program represent the best in training, in ability, and in patriotism. They are not satisfied with the progress thus far made. None of us will be satisfied until the job is done.

No matter whether the original goal was set too high or too low, our objective is quicker and better results. To give you two illustrations:

Appendix A FDR's Four Freedoms Speech 5A

We are behind schedule in turning out finished airplanes; we are working day and night to solve the innumerable problems and to catch up.

We are ahead of schedule in building warships but we are working to get even further ahead of that schedule.

To change a whole nation from a basis of peacetime production of implements of peace to a basis of wartime production of implements of war is no small task. And the greatest difficulty comes at the beginning of the program, when new tools, new plant facilities, new assembly lines, and new ship ways must first be constructed before the actual materiel begins to flow steadily and speedily from them.

The Congress, of course, must rightly keep itself informed at all times of the progress of the program. However, there is certain information, as the Congress itself will readily recognize, which, in the interests of our own security and those of the nations that we are supporting, must of needs be kept in confidence.

New circumstances are constantly begetting new needs for our safety. I shall ask this Congress for greatly increased new appropriations and authorizations to carry on what we have begun.

I also ask this Congress for authority and for funds sufficient to manufacture additional munitions and war supplies of many kinds, to be turned over to those nations which are now in actual war with aggressor nations.

Our most useful and immediate role is to act as an arsenal for them as well as for ourselves. They do not need man power, but they do need billions of dollars' worth of the weapons of defense.

The time is near when they will not be able to pay for them all in ready cash. We cannot, and we will not, tell them that they must surrender, merely because of present inability to pay for the weapons which we know they must have.

I do not recommend that we make them a loan of dollars with which to pay for these weapons loan to be repaid in dollars.

I recommend that we make it possible for those nations to continue to obtain war materials in the United States, fitting their orders into our own program. Nearly all their materiel would, if the time ever came, be useful for our own defense.

Taking counsel of expert military and naval authorities, considering what is best for our own security, we are free to decide how much should be kept here and how much should be sent abroad to our friends who by their

Appendix A FDR's Four Freedoms Speech 6A

determined and heroic resistance are giving us time in which to make ready our own defense.

For what we send abroad, we shall be repaid within a reasonable time following the close of hostilities, in similar materials, or, at our option, in other goods of many kinds, which they can produce and which we need.

Let us say to the democracies: "We Americans are vitally concerned in your defense of freedom. We are putting forth our energies, our resources and our organizing powers to give you the strength to regain and maintain a free world. We shall send you, in ever-increasing numbers, ships, planes, tanks, guns. This is our purpose and our pledge."

In fulfillment of this purpose we will not be intimidated by the threats of dictators that they will regard as a breach of international law or as an act of war our aid to the democracies which dare to resist their aggression. Such aid is not an act of war, even if a dictator should unilaterally proclaim it so to be.

When the dictators, if the dictators, are ready to make war upon us, they will not wait for an act of war on our part. They did not wait for Norway or Belgium or the Netherlands to commit an act of war.

Their only interest is in a new one-way international law, which lacks mutuality in its observance, and, therefore, becomes an instrument of oppression.

The happiness of future generations of Americans may well depend upon how effective and how immediate we can make our aid felt. No one can tell the exact character of the emergency situations that we may be called upon to meet. The Nation's hands must not be tied when the Nation's life is in danger.

We must all prepare to make the sacrifices that the emergency-almost as serious as war itself demands. Whatever stands in the way of speed and efficiency in defense preparations must give way to the national need.

A free nation has the right to expect full cooperation from all groups. A free nation has the right to look to the leaders of business, of labor, and of agriculture to take the lead in stimulating effort, not among other groups but within their own groups.

The best way of dealing with the few slackers or trouble makers in our midst is, first, to shame them by patriotic example, and, if that fails, to use the sovereignty of Government to save Government.

Appendix A FDR's Four Freedoms Speech 7A

As men do not live by bread alone, they do not fight by armaments alone. Those who man our defenses, and those behind them who build our defenses, must have the stamina and the courage which come from unshakable belief in the manner of life which they are defending. The mighty action that we are calling for cannot be based on a disregard of all things worth fighting for.

The Nation takes great satisfaction and much strength from the things which have been done to make its people conscious of their individual stake in the preservation of democratic life in America. Those things have toughened the fiber of our people, have renewed their faith and strengthened their devotion to the institutions we make ready to protect.

Certainly this is no time for any of us to stop thinking about the social and economic problems which are the root cause of the social revolution which is today a supreme factor in the world.

For there is nothing mysterious about the foundations of a healthy and strong democracy. The basic things expected by our people of their political and economic systems are simple. They are:

Equality of opportunity for youth and for others.
Jobs for those who can work.
Security for those who need it.
The ending of special privilege for the few.
The preservation of civil liberties for all.

The enjoyment of the fruits of scientific progress in a wider and constantly rising standard of living.

These are the simple, basic things that must never be lost sight of in the turmoil and unbelievable complexity of our modern world. The inner and abiding strength of our economic and political systems is dependent upon the degree to which they fulfill these expectations.

Many subjects connected with our social economy call for immediate improvement.
As examples:

We should bring more citizens under the coverage of old-age pensions and unemployment insurance.

We should widen the opportunities for adequate medical care.

We should plan a better system by which persons deserving or needing gainful employment may obtain it.

I have called for personal sacrifice. I am assured of the willingness of almost all Americans to respond to that call.

Appendix A FDR's Four Freedoms Speech 8A

A part of the sacrifice means the payment of more money in taxes. In my Budget Message I shall recommend that a greater portion of this great defense program be paid for from taxation than we are paying today. No person should try, or be allowed, to get rich out of this program; and the principle of tax payments in accordance with ability to pay should be constantly before our eyes to guide our legislation.

If the Congress maintains these principles, the voters, putting patriotism ahead of pocketbooks, will give you their applause.

In the future days, which we seek to make secure, we look forward to a world founded upon four essential human freedoms.

The first is freedom of speech and expression everywhere in the world.

The second is freedom of every person to worship God in his own way everywhere in the world.

The third is freedom from want which, translated into world terms, means economic understandings which will secure to every nation a healthy peacetime life for its inhabitants-everywhere in the world.

The fourth is freedom from fear which, translated into world terms, means a world-wide reduction of armaments to such a point and in such a thorough fashion that no nation will be in a position to commit an act of physical aggression against any neighbor anywhere in the world.

That is no vision of a distant millennium. It is a definite basis for a kind of world attainable in our own time and generation. That kind of world is the very antithesis of the so-called new order of tyranny which the dictators seek to create with the crash of a bomb.

To that new order we oppose the greater conception the moral order. A good society is able to face schemes of world domination and foreign revolutions alike without fear.

Since the beginning of our American history, we have been engaged in change in a perpetual peaceful revolution a revolution which goes on steadily, quietly adjusting itself to changing conditions without the concentration camp or the quick-lime in the ditch. The world order which we seek is the cooperation of free countries, working together in a friendly, civilized society.

Appendix A FDR's Four Freedoms Speech 9A

This nation has placed its destiny in the hands and heads and hearts of its millions of free men and women; and its faith in freedom under the guidance of God. Freedom means the supremacy of human rights everywhere. Our support goes to those who struggle to gain those rights or keep them. Our strength is our unity of purpose. To that high concept there can be no end save victory.

Made in the USA
San Bernardino, CA
11 June 2014